アントニン・レーモンド

チャーチ＆チャペル

日本
1935〜1970

解説｜内藤恒方、土屋重文　　撮影｜宮本和義

Antonin Raymond
Church & Chapel
Japan
1935〜1970

Text:Tsunekata Naitou, Shigebumi Tsuchiya
Photos:Kazuyoshi Miyamoto

Banana Books

写真提供：レーモンド設計事務所

アントニン・レーモンドと妻ノエミ・1965年

Antonin and Noémi Raymond.1965
Photo credit:Raymond Architectural Design Office

目次

軽井沢聖ポール教会 ──────────────── 004
聖アンセルモカトリック目黒教会 ─────────── 011
レーモンド設計事務所での経験と学んだこと ──── 内藤恒方 022
神言神学院 ─────────────────── 028
クリスチャン・アカデミー音楽堂 ──────────── 038
「建築家は60歳になって一人前！」と彼は言った ── 土屋重文 044
クリスチャン・アカデミー音楽堂のことども ───── 土屋重文 060

アントニン・レーモンド
チャーチ＆チャペル
日本

Antonin Raymond
Church & Chapel

Contents

St. Paul's Catholic Church ─────────────── 004
St. Anselms' Meguro Church ─────────────── 011
Experiences and Learning at Raymond Architectural Design Office ─── 023
Divine Word Seminary Chapel ─────────────── 028
Christian Academy's Music Auditorium ───────────── 038
He said, "An architect is full-fledged when he is 60." ────── 045
Regarding the Christian Academy Music Auditorium ──────── 061

軽井沢 聖ポール教会 ［現・軽井沢聖パウロカトリック教会］ 長野県軽井沢・1935

St.Paul's Catholic Church/Karuizawa/1935

▼南側正面外観　レーモンドの故郷・チェコの木造教会を彷彿とさせるが、モダニズムの香りがする。

Exterior of the south side front: This has a resemblance to a wooden church in Raymond's old home, the Czech Republic, but also has an atmosphere of modernism.

▲北側外観　創建当時は杮葺きの屋根であった。　Exterior of north side: When it was first built, it had a shingled roof.

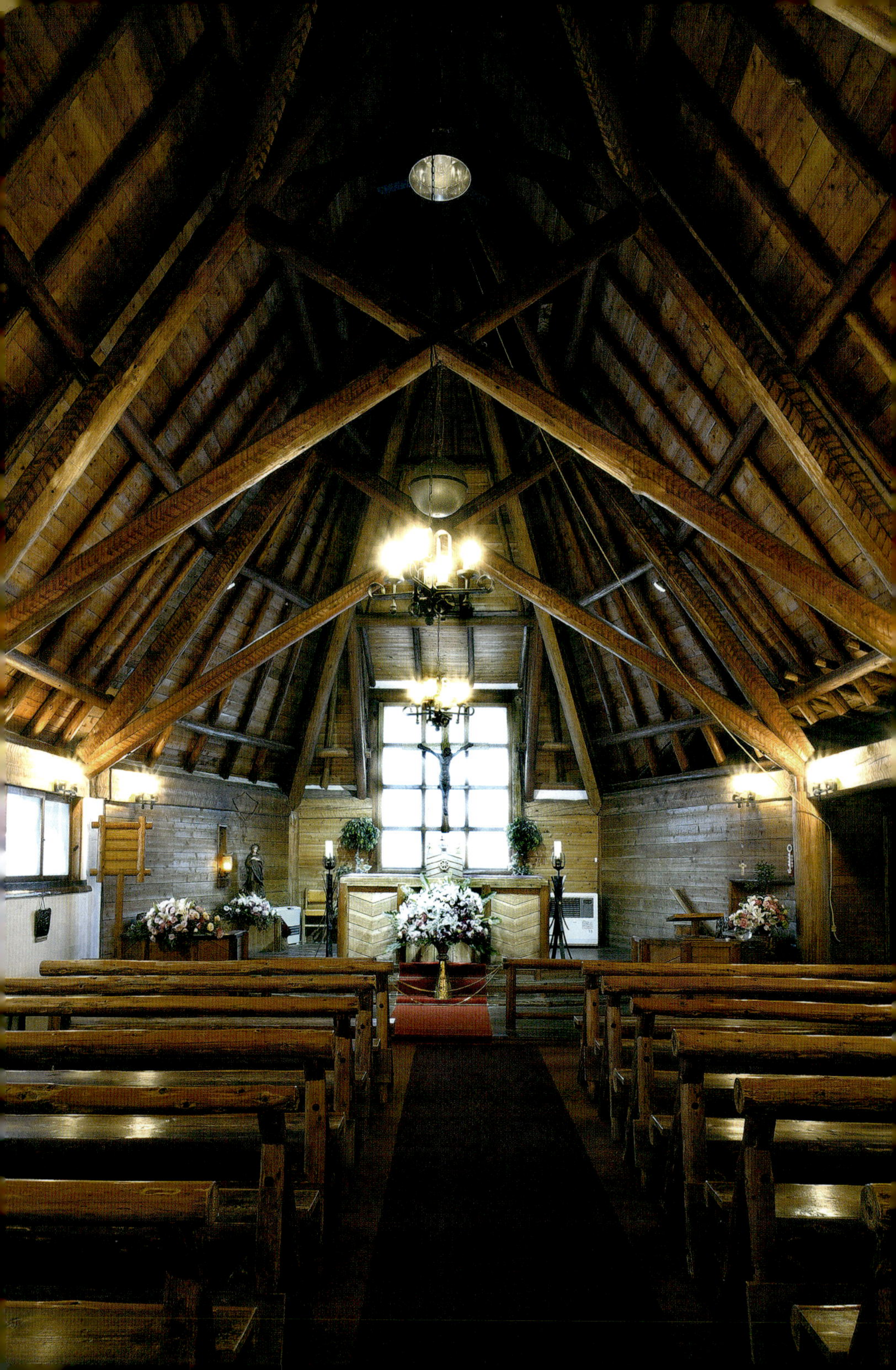

▲聖堂内部　小さなパイプオルガンと懺悔室もある。

Inside of the church: There is also a small pipe organ and a confession booth.

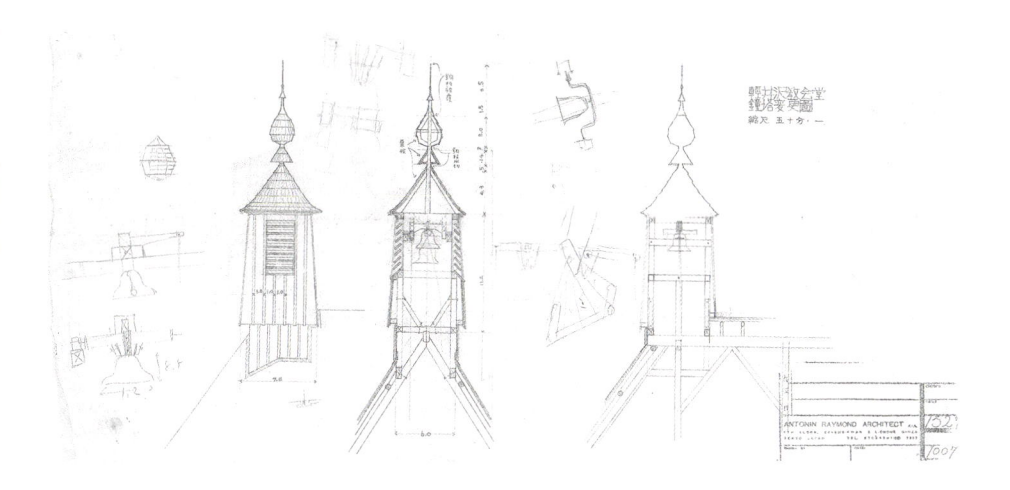

◀聖堂内部　地元の大工たちの話に耳を傾けながらつくられたダイナミックな木造架構。長刃の後もすがすがしい、木造モダニズム。

Inside of the church: The dynamic wooden framework was made while listening to the local carpenters' stories. The wooden modernist building with brisk marks made by long-blade.

007

◀ 2階に上る木造回り階段　模様は夫人ノエミさんのデザイン。

Wooden geometric stairs to the second floor: The pattern was his wife Noémi's design.

▼ ざっくりしたつくりの丸太長椅子が80年の祈りを支えている。

Roughly made log benches have been supporting prayers for 80 years.

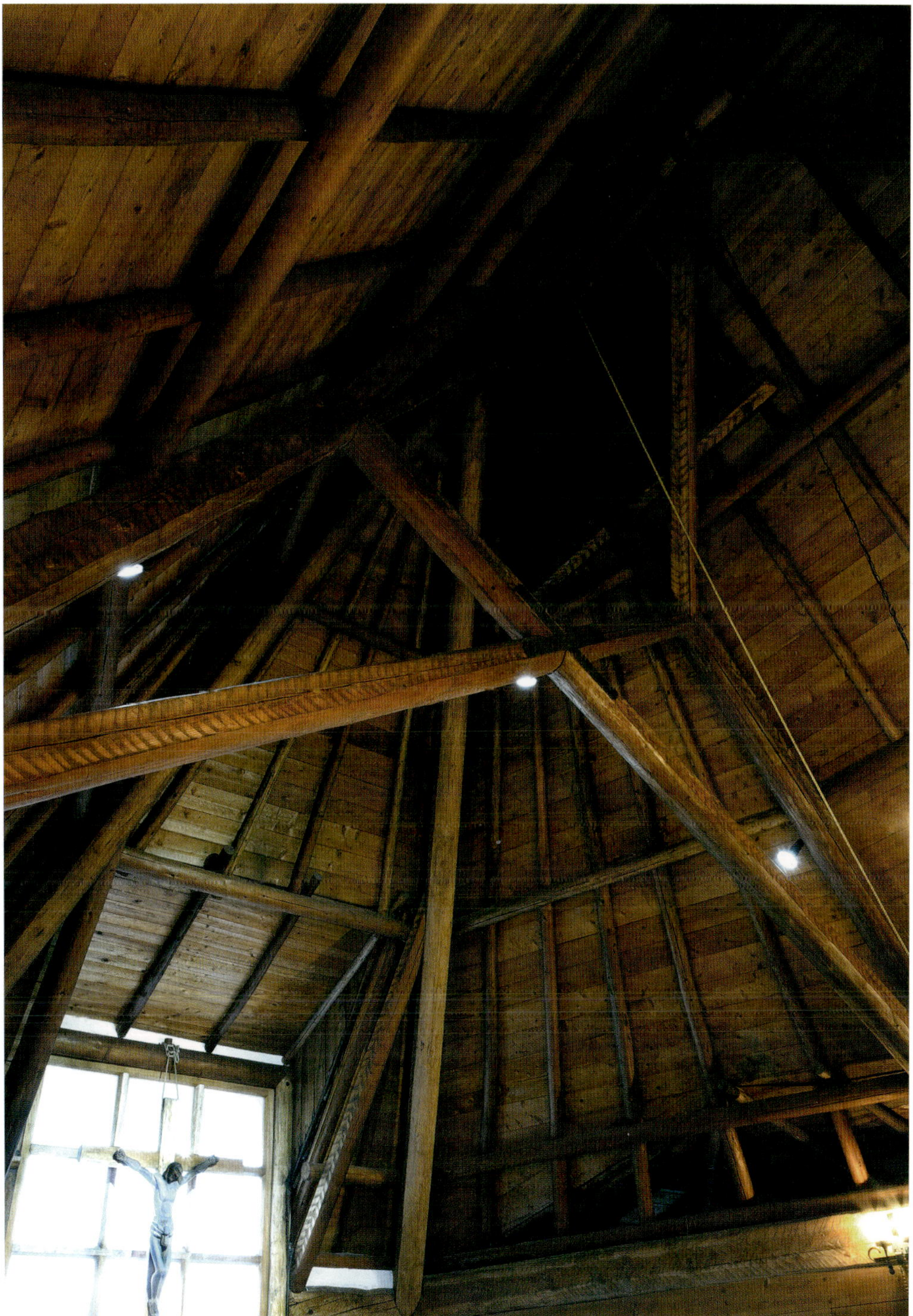

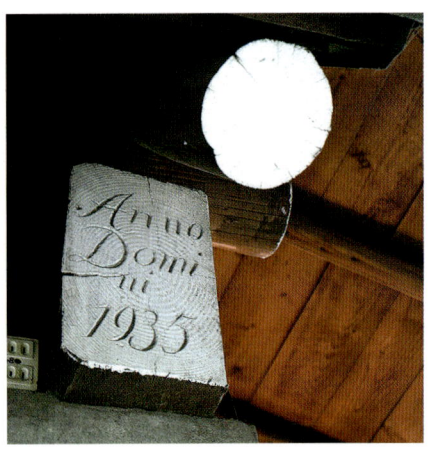

◀竣工年を記された梁

Beam with the completion year written on it

聖アンセルモカトリック目黒教会

東京都目黒・1954

St. Anselm's Meguro Church/Tokyo/1954

教会内部　モダンな金箔の天蓋と十字架。円をモチーフにした背景との敬虔なアート。

Inside of the church: Modern golden pedestal and cross. They make devout art along with the background that has circles as a motif.

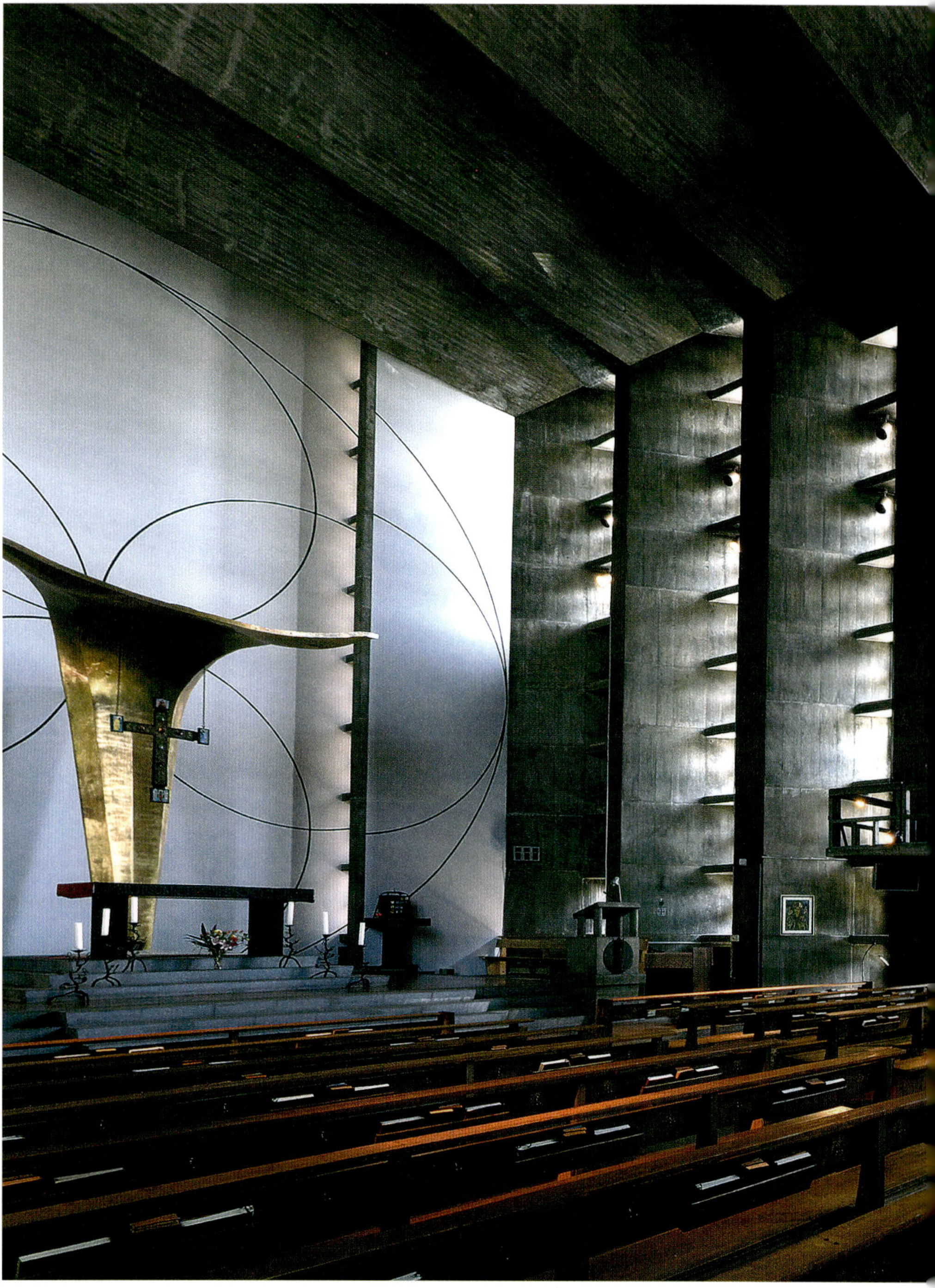

▲マッシブなコンクリート打放しと側壁から入る自然光が暖かで静謐な祈りの空間をつくる。

Massive as-cast concrete and natural light from the side wall create the warm and peaceful space for praying.

▲聖堂内の最後部にあるアプス(後陣)は洗礼堂　The apse in the back of the church is a baptistery.

◀祭壇の対向にはステンドグラスとパイプオルガン

Stained-glass and pipe organ opposite to the altar.

▲コンクリート打放しの朗読台　As-cast concrete lectern.

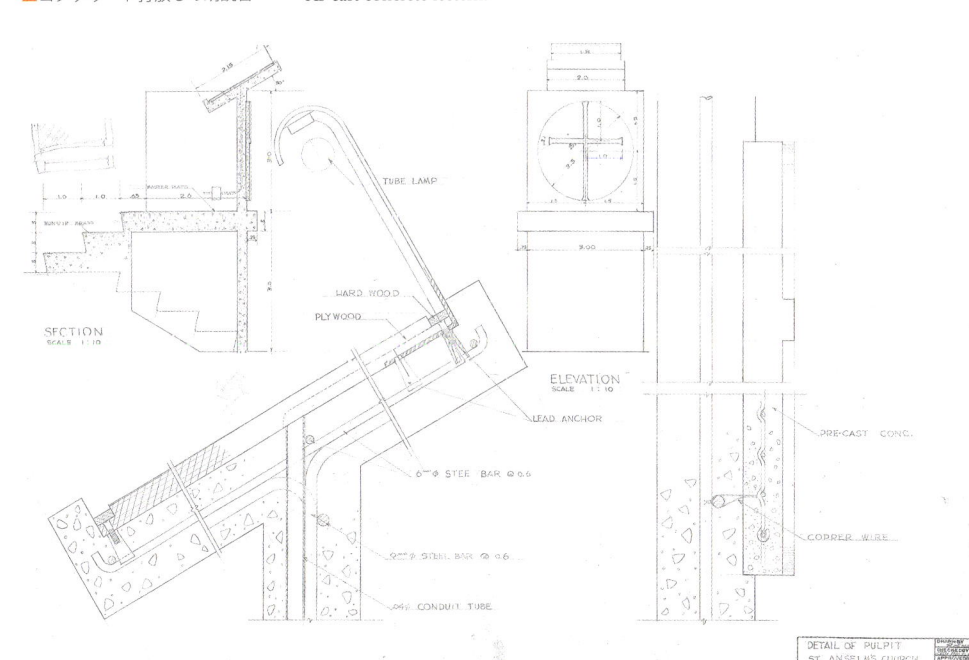

▲無柱空間を支える曲面折版天井
◀2階への階段。軽井沢の聖ポール教会を思わせる。

▲ Folded-plate structured ceiling supports the space without pillars.
◀ Staircase to the second floor, which reminds us of St. Paul's Catholic Church in Karuizawa

▶各側壁にはキリストの「十字架への道行」の14モチーフがノエミ夫人によってデザインされた。

On each side wall, Noémi designed the 14 motifs from Christ's "Way of the Cross"

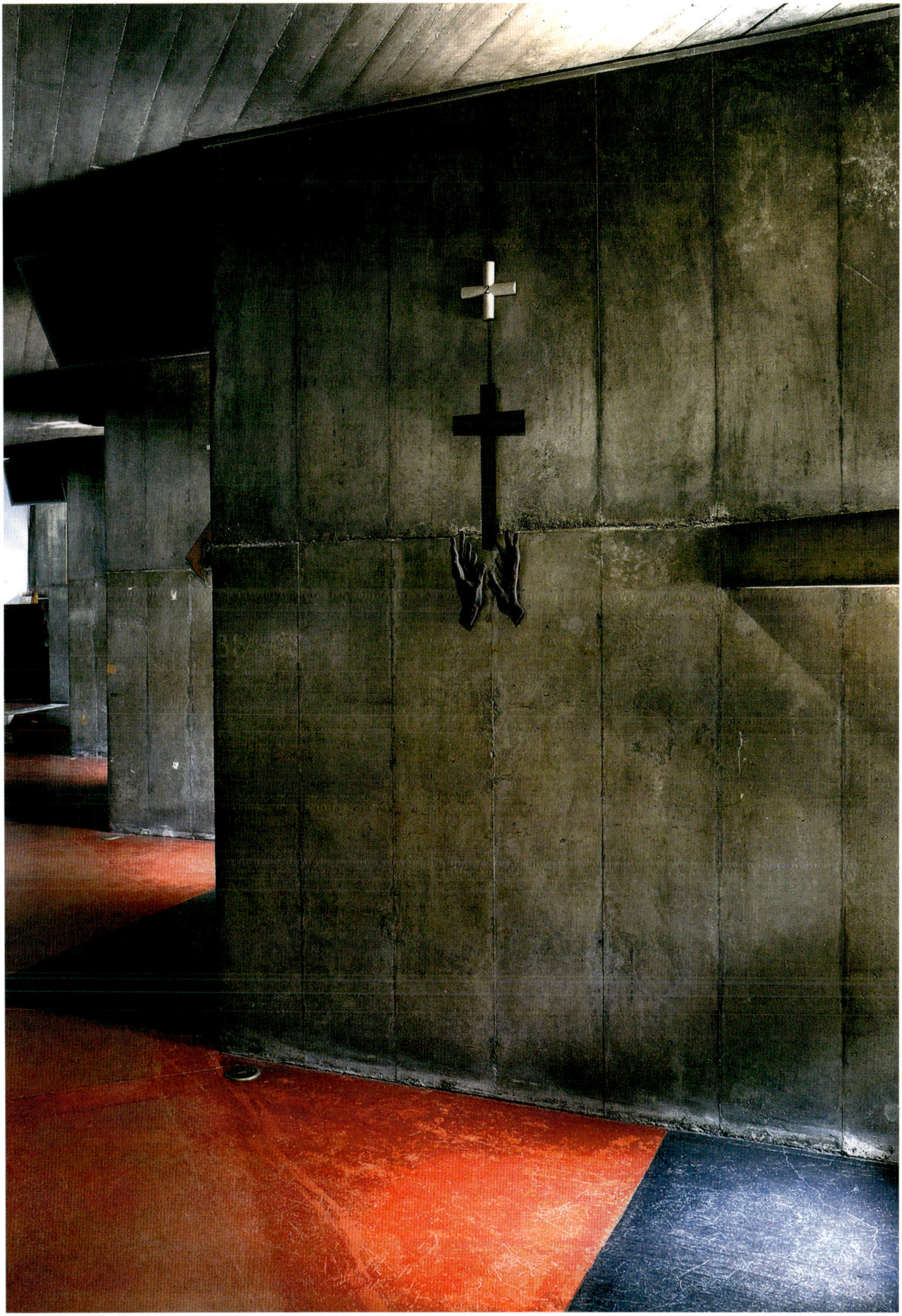

018

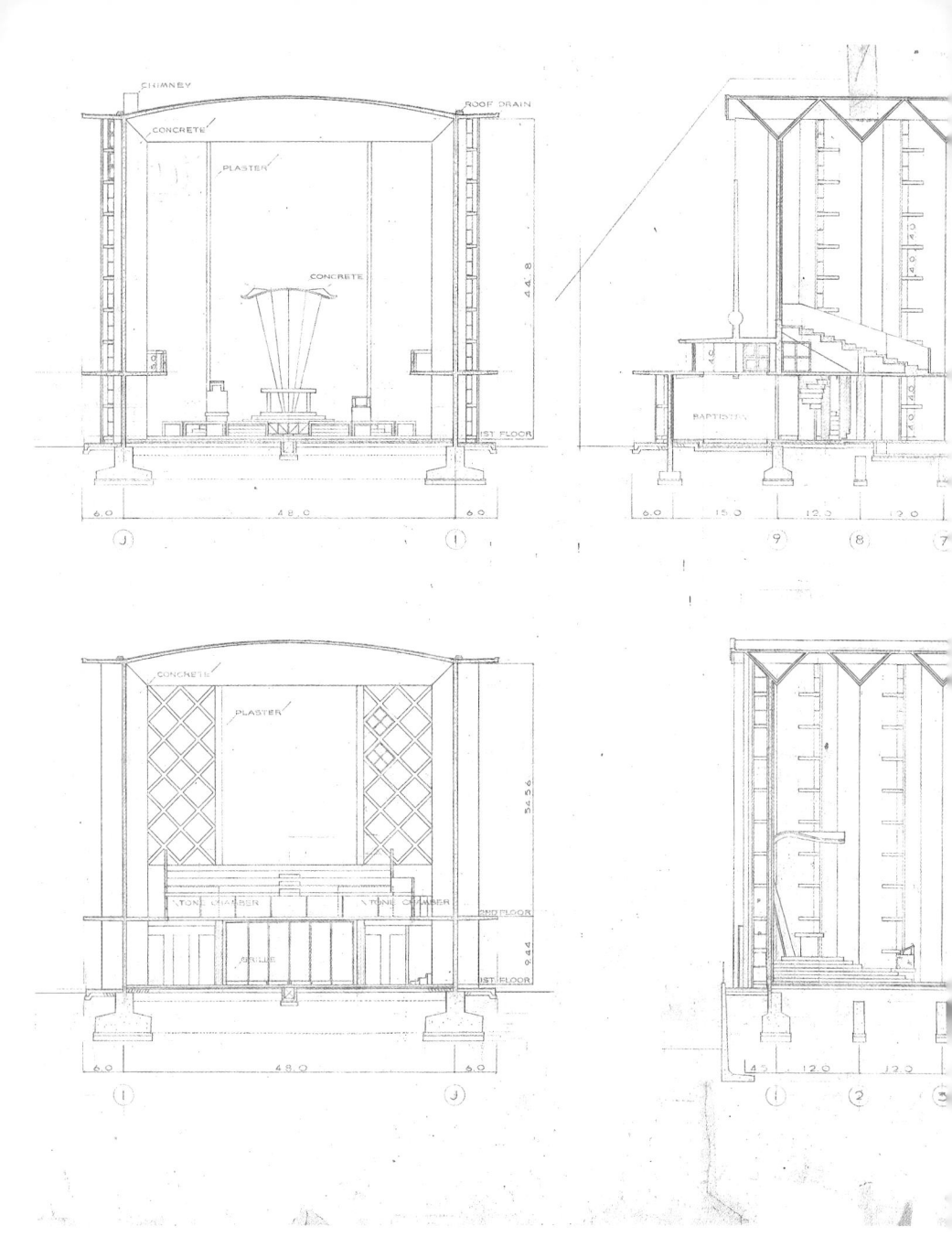

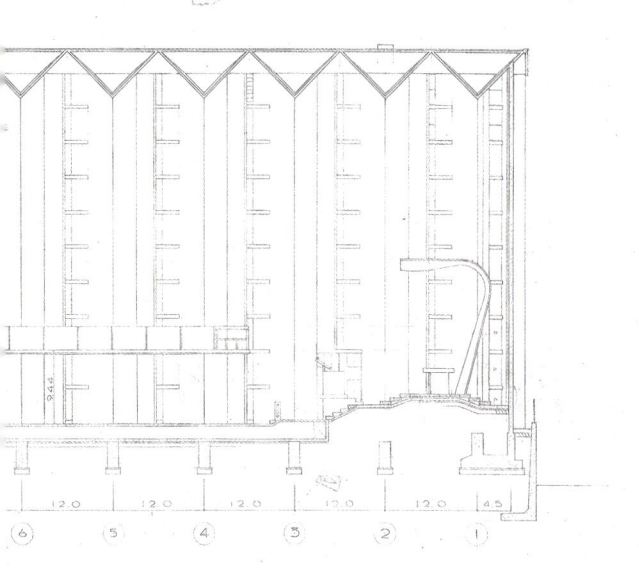

▲燭台と御影石のプレート

Candleholders and granite plate

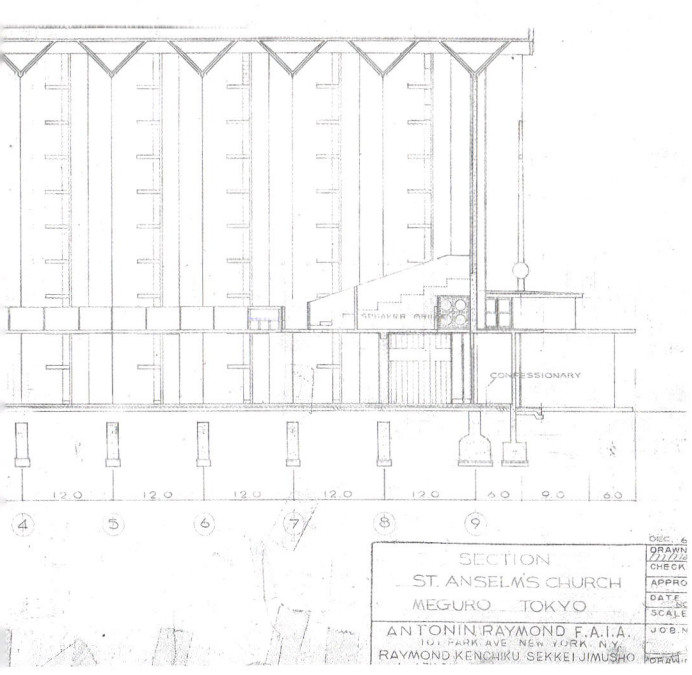

SECTION
ST. ANSELM'S CHURCH
MEGURO — TOKYO
ANTONIN RAYMOND F.A.I.A.
101 PARK AVE. NEW YORK. N.Y.
RAYMOND KENCHIKU SEKKEI JIMUSHO

▲鍛鉄とサビ鉄でつくられた「十字架への道行」

"the stations of the cross" made of wrought iron and rusty iron

019

▲側壁に設けられたサイドライト採り

Side lighting windows on the side walls.

◀南東側外観　前面道路は狭く、狭い敷地の中に教会、寄宿舎、事務棟、図書館、幼稚園がはめ込まれている。教会の平面は 15.1m × 30.3m

Exterior of the south east side: Facing toward a narrow road. On the small site, the church, residential hall, office building, library, and kindergarten are arranged. The church floor area is 15.1m x 30.3m.

▲南側見上げ　屋根版の薄さがきわだつ。

Looking up from the south side: The thinness of the roof materials stands out.

レーモンド設計事務所での経験と学んだこと
二つの教会の設計を含めて

内藤恒方

1958年から63年まで、私はレーモンド設計事務所に働くことができた。東京芸大の建築科を卒業して、23歳から28歳までの5年間である。レーモンドさんは70歳、私が退社した時は75歳で、まだまだ元気で精力的にお仕事をされている時期である。

入社した4月1日に、レーモンドさんが私の席にこられ、白い紙の貼られた製図版の上に、
"Architect should put chaos into order"
と書かれたことは、一生忘れることはできない。建築家として基本的な考え方、フィロソフィーを第一日目に直接教えられたことは、たいへんに幸せであった。

同年の夏に、その年入社した2人、A君と私はレーモンド夫妻と3ヶ月の間、軽井沢で合宿して設計の仕事をすることができたことは、有益なことであった。まだ軽井沢の「新スタジオ」ができる前で、旧軽井沢の入り口付近に、小さな戸建の家を2軒借りて、一戸にはレーモンド夫妻、一戸には我々二人が寝泊まりした。朝昼晩の食事を夫妻とともにしながらの合宿は忘れられない経験である。東京の事務所のレーモンドさんの顔とは違った、ジョークを話しながら、ユーモアたっぷりの優しい顔を知ることができた。

ここでの私の仕事は、群馬音楽センターのホワイエの左右にある回り階段の図面をつくること。いろいろなスケッチが持ち込まれ、手摺りのディテール、ハンドレールを掘り込みにする案など数々のスタディがなされた。

最終的には、コンクリートの腰壁に円形の孔を開けた形になり、それらをリズムを持たせながらつなぐ目地を入れたデザインに落ち着くまでの過程に多くの時間を要した。このデザインにはOrderが感じられるものであった。

東京の事務所にもどり、事務所の一員になり、Bさんのチームに入れられ、四国にある町役場の設計図面を書くことになった。事務所では、レーモンドさんは自分自身の確固としたフィロソフィーの基にデザインをすすめていく建築家であったが、Bさんは、このルールを無視して自分の判断の基に仕事をすすめ、いつもレーモンドさんと大争いになった。結果としてOrderのないChaosの状態のまま仕事は終わり、皆、Unhappyな結末である。建築家とは、社会に貢献するための職業であり、プロフェッショナルとして、何かが起こった時には、その責任をとらなければならないという意思の表現を感じとることができた。

いろいろな経験の時間が流れ、数々の仕事をした中で私が関わった教会の設計の仕事は二つある。1958年〜59年、東京郊外の三鷹にある国際キリスト教大学の教会の改築の仕事。世田谷区若林にある日本聖公会の聖十字教会の新しい設計の仕事は、1960年から61年の時期である。

国際キリスト教大学の教会は、他の建築

Experiences and Learning at Raymond Architectural Design Office
Including Designs of Two Churches

Tsunekata Naito

From 1958 to 1963, I had the opportunity to work for the Raymond Architectural Design Office. It was for five years from ages 23 to 28 years old, after I graduated from Tokyo University of the Arts, Department of Architecture. Mr. Raymond was 70 years old when I started, and was 75 when I left. He was still in good health and energetically working during that time.

I can never forget that Mr. Raymond came to my desk on the day I started working, April 1st, and wrote "Architect should put chaos into order" on white paper stuck on my drawing board. It was a very fortunate that I was directly taught this basic way of thinking of an architect as well as a philosophy on my first day of work.

It was very beneficial that two of the newly-starting workers that year, Mr. A and I, stayed and worked in Karuizawa for three months in the summer of the same year with Mr. and Mrs. Raymond. It was before the "New Studio" in Karuizawa was built, and we rented two small detached houses near the entrance of Kyukaruizawa. Mr. and Mrs. Raymond stayed in one of the houses and the two of us stayed in the other. The experience of this training camp, in which we ate every meal with Mr. and Mrs. Raymond, is unforgettable. He told us jokes and we were able to see the humorous and kind side of Mr. Raymond, which was different from when he was at the office in Tokyo.

◻My task there was to make a plan for geometric stairs located on the left and right sides of the foyer in the Gunma Music Center. Various sketches were brought in and numerous studies were conducted on details of the banisters, ideas for carving handrails, etc.

In the end, its form was decided to be a concrete waist-high wall with round holes. The process to confirm the design, in which holes were connected with joints while creating rhythms, took a long time. In this design, existence of the order can be felt.

We went back to the office in Tokyo and became office workers. I joined Mr. B's team to design a town hall in Shikoku. At the office, Mr. Raymond was an architect who designed his work based on his own solid philosophy; however, Mr. B ignored this rule and performed his work based on his own decisions, and always had big arguments with Mr. Raymond. As a result, the design work ended in chaos without any order, and everyone was unhappy. I sensed an expression of his resolve that an architect is in a profession that contributes to society, and has to be responsible as a professional when something happens.

As time passed I experienced a variety of things. I was involved in two church designs among the numerous projects I worked on. One was from 1958 to 1959, a renovation project of a church in the International Christian University (ICU), located in Mitaka, a suburb of Tokyo. The other one was from 1960 to 1961, a new design for the Holy Cross Church, of the Anglican

▲東京・若林に建つ聖十字教会。集成材とラワン合板のローコスト建築だが凛とした祈りの空間をつくっている。

The Holy Cross Anglican Episcopal Church in Wakabayashi, Tokyo: Although it is a low-cost building made with laminated lumber and lauan plywood, a dignified space for praying is created.

家の設計によって既に建設されていたものである。『自伝アントニン・レーモンド』(鹿島出版会刊)によると、「かつての飛行場の跡地の整理に、先任建築家の無秩序で弱気な結果、新しい建物はでたらめに配置され、教会のような植民地スタイル……」と記されている。実際には、主として両側の壁面にスリット状の窓をつくり、祭壇に向かって陽が入るようにした。大学は後日、祭壇に大きなパイプオルガンを置き、レーモンドさんによる改築の意図を無視した状態になり、Chaosの結果に終わっている。

若林の聖十字教会は、飛行機の格納庫の架構のために開発された、ごく初期の集成

Episcopal Church in Japan, located in Wakabayashi, Setagaya-ku.

The church in the ICU had been designed and already built by another architect. According to "Antonin Raymond: An Autobiography" (Kajima Institute Publishing Co., Ltd.), he noted that "cluttered with remains of buildings, roads, water mains, drainage and other factory facilities, and with the rather unorganized and feeble efforts of the former architect….". Actually, for the most part, slit-shaped windows were created on walls on both sides to direct sunlight towards the altar. Later, the university set a large-sized pipe organ on the altar and ignored the intentions of Mr. Raymond's renovation, and it ended up as a chaotic result.

For the Holy Cross Anglican Episcopal Church in Wakabayashi, a primitive laminated lumber, which was developed for frameworks for aircraft hangars, was used for the frame. Then, lauan plywood was gradually curved and placed from the walls to the ceiling, and sky lights and vents were installed on the ceiling. In order to design a church for gathering people on a limited budget, and to create an amiable Japanese-style building, a lot of efforts were made.

It was finished by a unique method of the Raymond Architectural Design Office: the cheapest thin plywood was fixed at one-inch intervals on the base with brass nails. No paint was used in order to obtain beautiful colors by aging. For the walls on the entrance side, plastic panels were spray painted and sandwiched between two glass panes. This created the only colorful wall in this space that looked like stained-glass. Milky-white ball-shaped lights were hung from the ceiling, and all were fixed in multiple directions with wires to prevent them from moving.

For the altar, there were simply a table, candleholders, and a wooden cross. All of the pews, which allow people to kneel, were designed by the Raymond Office and were custom-made by a furniture manufacturer. They were made with lauan wood and were far from luxurious, but they were comfortable

材を骨組みとし、それにラワン合板を少しずつ曲げて壁から天井まで貼り、天井部分にトップライトと換気装置が施されている。予算の少ない仕事で、人々の集まる教会をどのようにしてつくるか、それも日本的な建築として親しまれるかなどについて努力がなされた。

薄い、一番安いベニヤ板を1インチ間隔に真鍮釘で下地に留める、レーモンド事務所独自の仕上げになっている。塗装はいっさい施さずに、経年変化によって美しい色合いになる仕上げである。入口側の壁面はプラスティック板にスプレーペイントをかけ、両面をガラスで挟み、ステンドグラスのようにしている。この空間で唯一のカラフルな壁面を作りだしている。照明は丸い球形の乳白色のボールが天井から吊り下げられ、揺れを防ぐためにすべてがワイヤーで四方に留められた。

祭壇も簡素にテーブルと燭台、木製の十字架があるだけである。ひざまずくことができる椅子、ピューはすべてレーモンド事務所で図面をおこし、家具屋さんで特別に製作された。ラワン材でつくられ、豪華とはとてもいえないが、教会での敬虔な礼拝の時を過ごすには快適なものとなっている。

2000年に聖十字教会は築40年になった。いろいろな不都合な個所が出てきて、修理・改築が必要になり、レーモンド事務所に問い合わせをし、私が担当であったことから私のところに相談があった。

それは、①老朽化により物理的な修理が必要な工事。前面の外壁が雨ざらしで取り換えが必要なことなど。②社会的な変化により、建築時には満足できたものが現在の人々の生活では対応できないこと。便所が男女別々に必要など。③その他。当初の設計時の趣旨を正確に守りながら、教会員の方々となんどか会合をもち、理解をふかめながら修理・改築をおこなった。

2012年には省エネ対策をはかるために、白熱灯の照明器具をLEDに変えた。この教会は、すべてオリジナルを守るために、細かい事まで問い合わせがあり、当初のOrderがいまだにきちんと守られている。

この二つの教会の設計を担当し、今日になって考えてみると、レーモンドさんの設計の作品には、いくつかのデザインの特色が見いだせる。

(1)住宅、教会、公共の建物などいずれも、日本的な雰囲気が漂っている。スケール感、仕上げ材とその使い方、テクスチャー、色、そして人間的な親しみやすさ。

(2)コンクリート造、打放しの面、さらに木造建築からは、手作りの感触が伝わってくること。建築を作った人、図面を作った人、考えた人、考えられた過程、すべてから手作りの感触が伝わってくる。

(3)建物を末永く使うことによって味が出てくること。修理を重ねながら使うことの素晴らしさ。レーモンド事務所の図面もそうであった。一度書いた図面は幾度も消しゴムで消しては書き直す、新しいトレペに書き直すことはしない。考えた過程が読み、分かるように。

(4)大きな架構による豊かな空間。F.L.ライトの空間との違い。

(5)建設費をミニマムにして作っていること。

これらは、私が事務所に入所した初日にレーモンドさんが製図版の白い紙に書いたOrderということであろう。

enough for pious church services.

In 2000, the Holy Cross Anglican Episcopal Church turned 40 years old. Many inconveniences appeared and the building required repair and renovation. Since I was in charge, the Raymond Office contacted me when the church contacted them.

Repair and renovation was for: (1) parts that physically required repair due to aging; for example, the front exterior walls were exposed to rain and required reinstallation, (2) parts that did not match present life styles due to social changes, even though needs had been satisfied when it was built; for example, separation of bathrooms for men and women, and (3) other items. The repair and renovation was conducted while accurately preserving the spirit of the original design, and deepening understanding through several meetings with church members.

In 2012, incandescent luminaires were changed to LEDs to save energy. In order to preserve the original state, this church asked about specific details and maintained the original order.

By working on these two church designs and thinking back on it now, several design characteristics of the architectural works of Mr. Raymond can be found:

(1) All of the buildings including houses, churches, and public buildings, have a Japanese-like atmosphere: scale, finishing materials and their use, texture, color, and a human friendliness.

(2) The handmade sense can be felt from the concrete structures, as their exposed concrete surfaces, to wooden buildings. Throughout everything, from the builders, the people who drew the plans and who made the plans, and the process of making the plans, every things handmade sense can be felt.

(3) The building's tastefulness deepens as it is used for a long time period: the beauty of using it by making repeated repairs. It was the same for the plans made in the Raymond Office. Once the plan was drawn, it was repeatedly erased and then redrawn. In order to show and understand the progression of thoughts, it was not redrawn on new tracing paper.

(4) Rich spaces with large-sized frames. The space differed from those by Frank Lloyd Wright.

(5) The building costs were minimized.

These might be the order that Mr. Raymond referred to when he wrote about it on white paper on my drawing board on my first day of work at his office.

神言神学院 愛知県名古屋・1964

Divine Word Seminary Chapel/Nagoya/1964

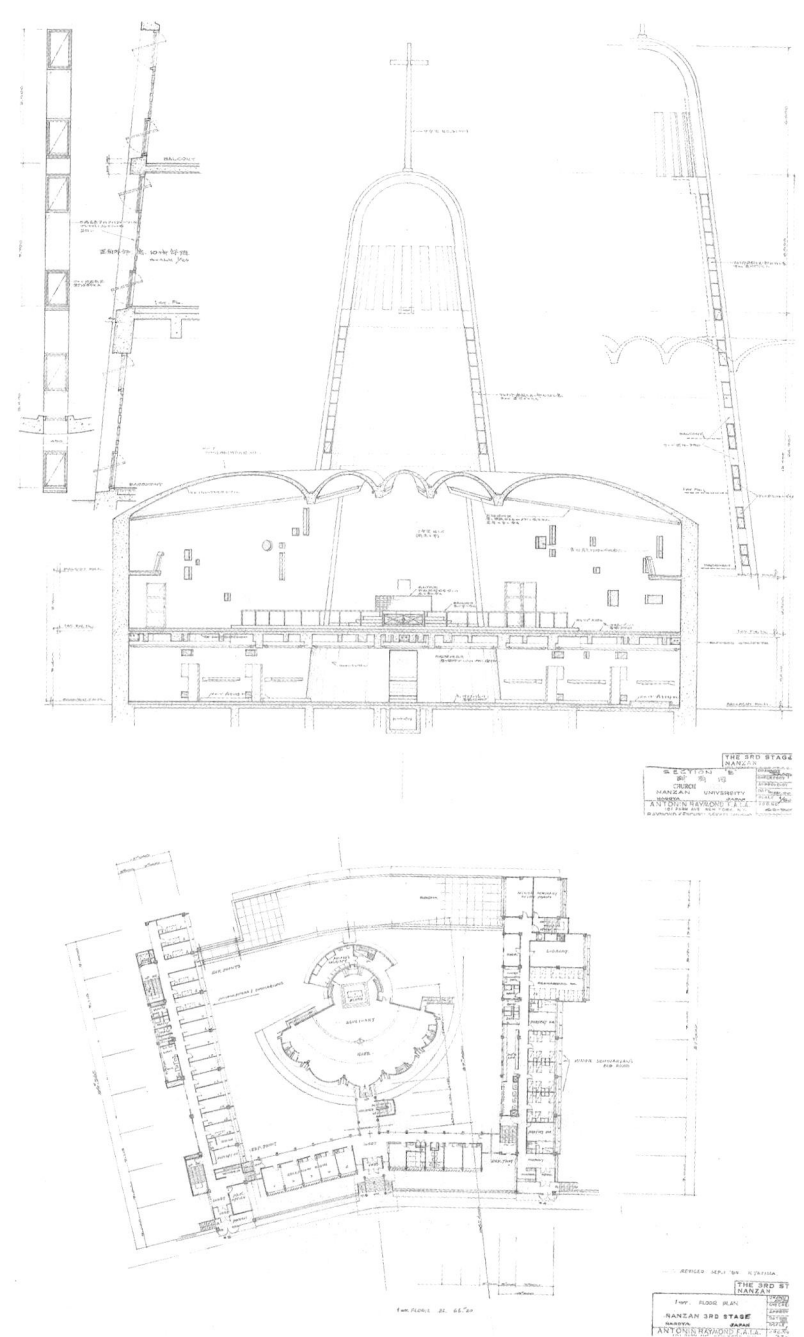

▲扇形の5つのシリンダーシェルと鐘楼はビザンチンの教会や東欧の初期ロマネスクの教会建築を思わせる。

Five of the fan-shaped cylinder shells and a bell tower reminds us of the Byzantine-style church buildings or early Romanesque church buildings in Eastern Europe.

029

▲4周を僧坊や教室や事務棟などが囲む修道院建築の中のチャペル。前面道路からは1.5層分ほど下がる。

Chapel is in a cloister building surrounded by monastery, classrooms, and office buildings. It is about one and a half stories lower than the road.

▲半階下がってエントランス。キャノピー、ルーバーが美しい。
▼半階上がった正面。

▲ Entrance hall is a half story down. It has a beautiful canopy and louvers.
▼ Front is a half story higher.

031

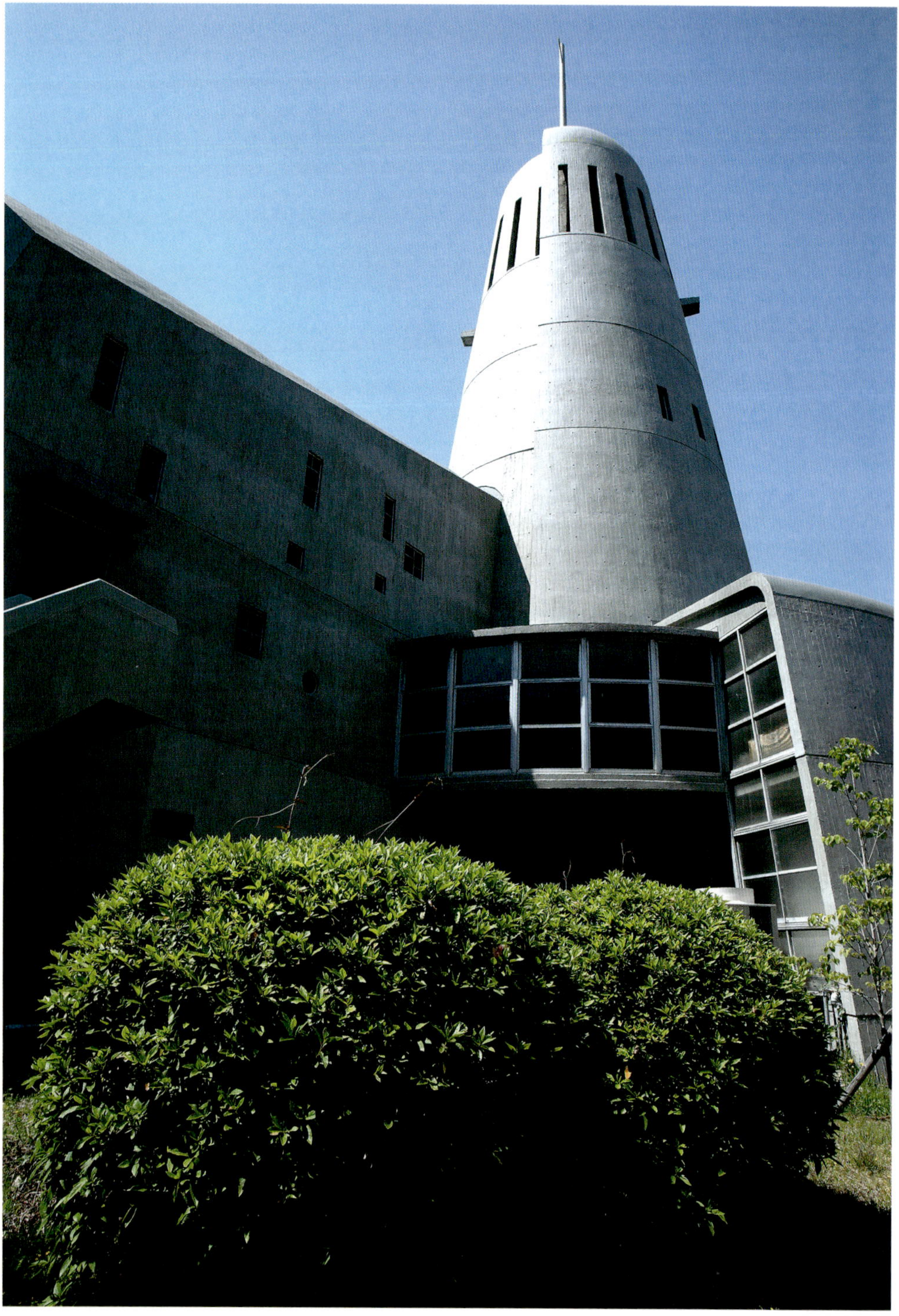

▲北壁に穿たれたさまざまな窓。
▶現代的なステンドグラスのデザイン。

▲ Variety of windows on the north wall.
▶ Modern stained-glass design.

◀南東見上げ。コルビュジエのモチーフで遊んでいる。

Looking up from the south east side. Being playful by using Le Corbusier's motif.

033

▲午後遅く、照明を落とした祭壇に聖なる光が降り注ぐ。
▼人工照明は円筒の谷部に隠され、照明器具は視野に入らない。

▲ In the late afternoon, holy light showers the dimly-lit alter.
▼ Artificial lights are hidden behind the cylinders, and lighting apparatus cannot be seen.

▶祭壇の上の鐘楼部分の開口がドラマチックな光を演出している。

On the upper part of the alter, the bell tower opening creates dramatic lighting.

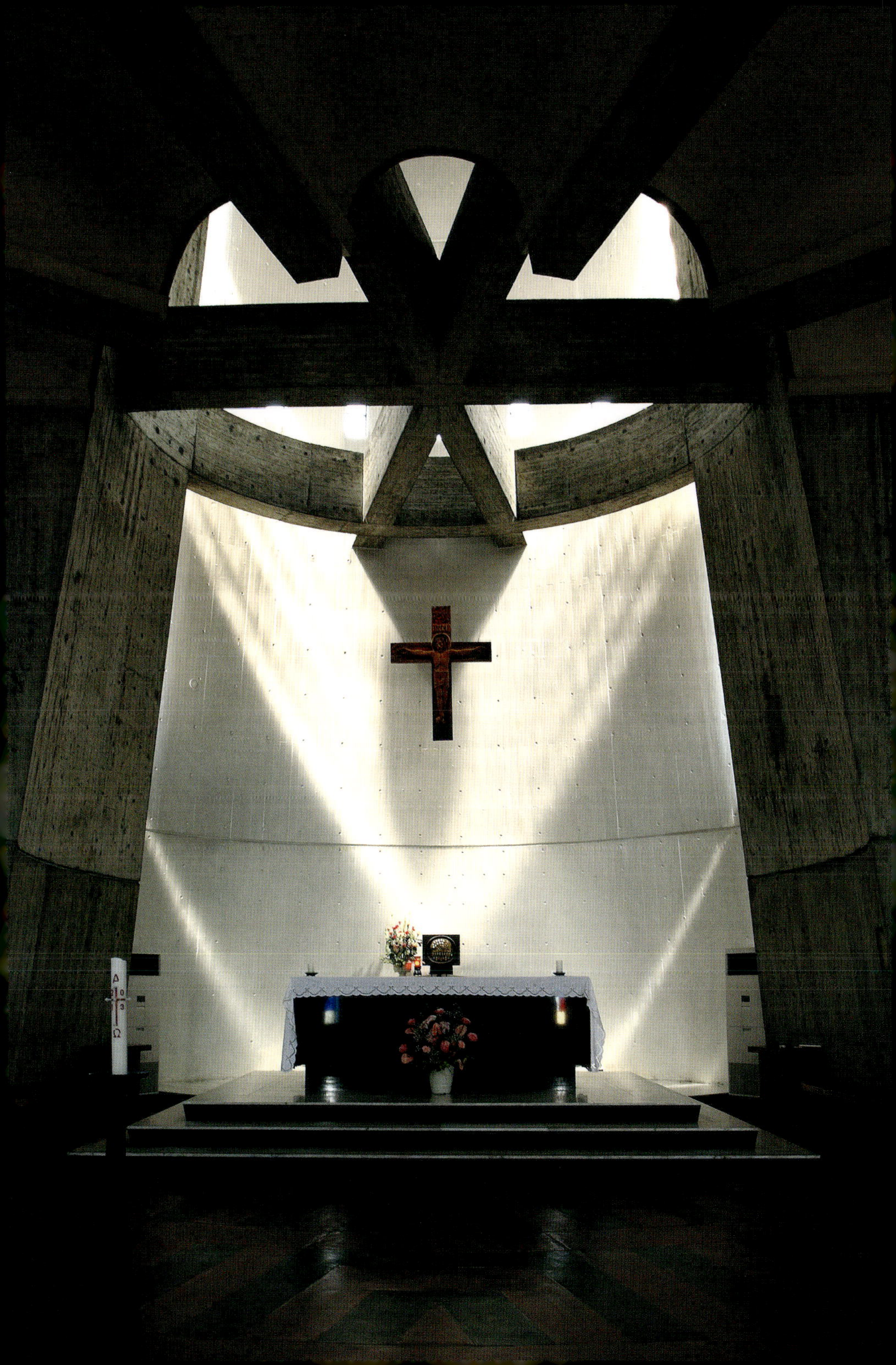

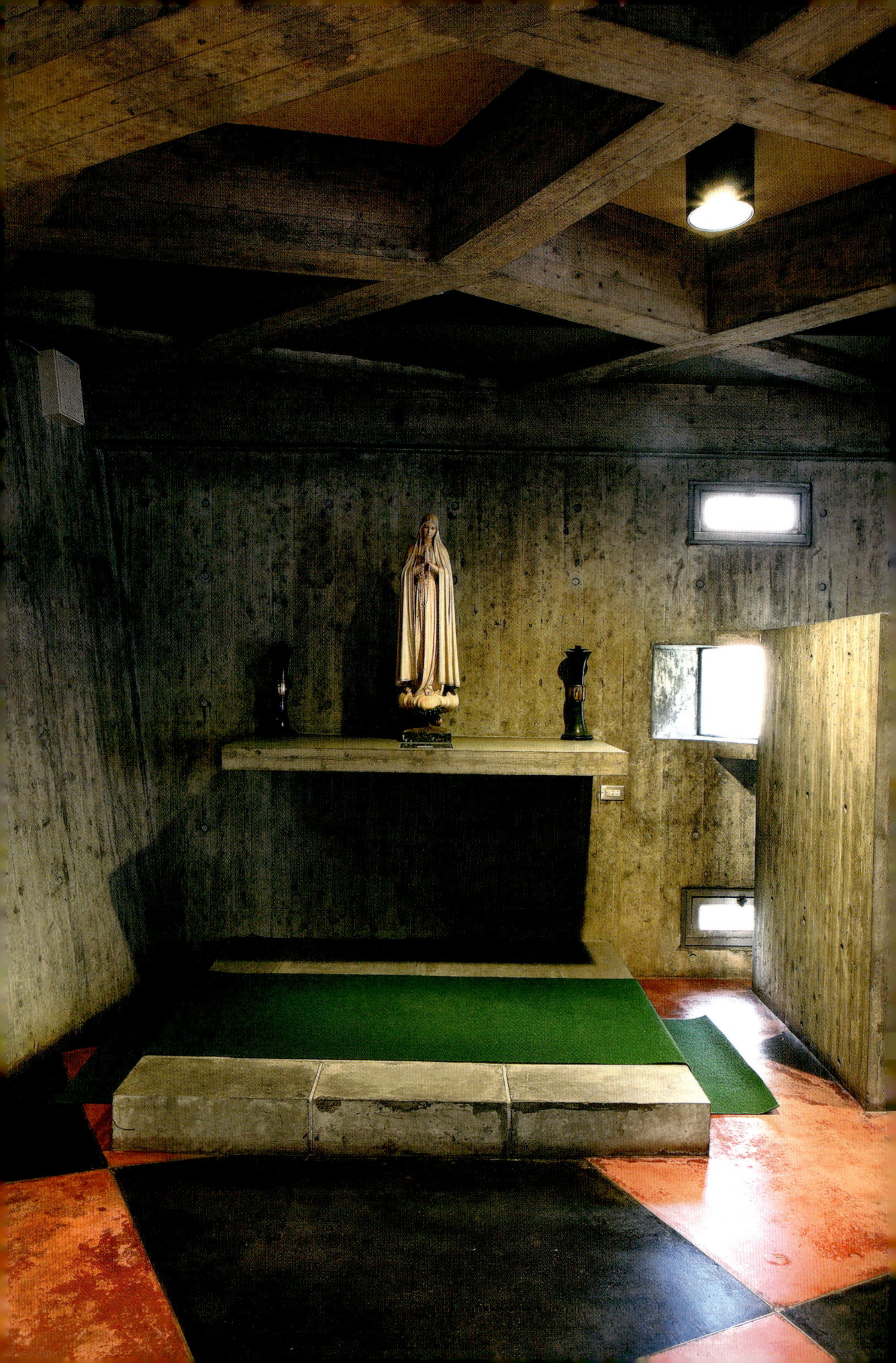

▲天井高の低い格子梁に囲われた
　静かな祈りの空間。
▶三角窓と礼拝コーナー

▲ Ceiling height of the underground chantry is low. A simple and quiet praying space, which is surrounded by lattice beams.
▶ Triangle window and church service space

◀地下の礼拝所に設けられた個別
　の礼拝スペース。

Underground chantry is for monks to pray and study. This is an individual space for praying.

037

クリスチャンアカデミー音楽堂

東京東久留米・1970

Christian Academy's Music Auditorium/Tokyo/1970

撮影：土屋重文

▲ 樹木にあわせて配置された音楽堂正面外観。季節に合わせて表情を変える。
◀ アカデミーのグランドから見た南面外観。

▲ Façade of the concert hall that was located by adjusting to the trees. It changes its expression as the seasons progress.
◀ Exterior of east side from the grounds of the academy.

038

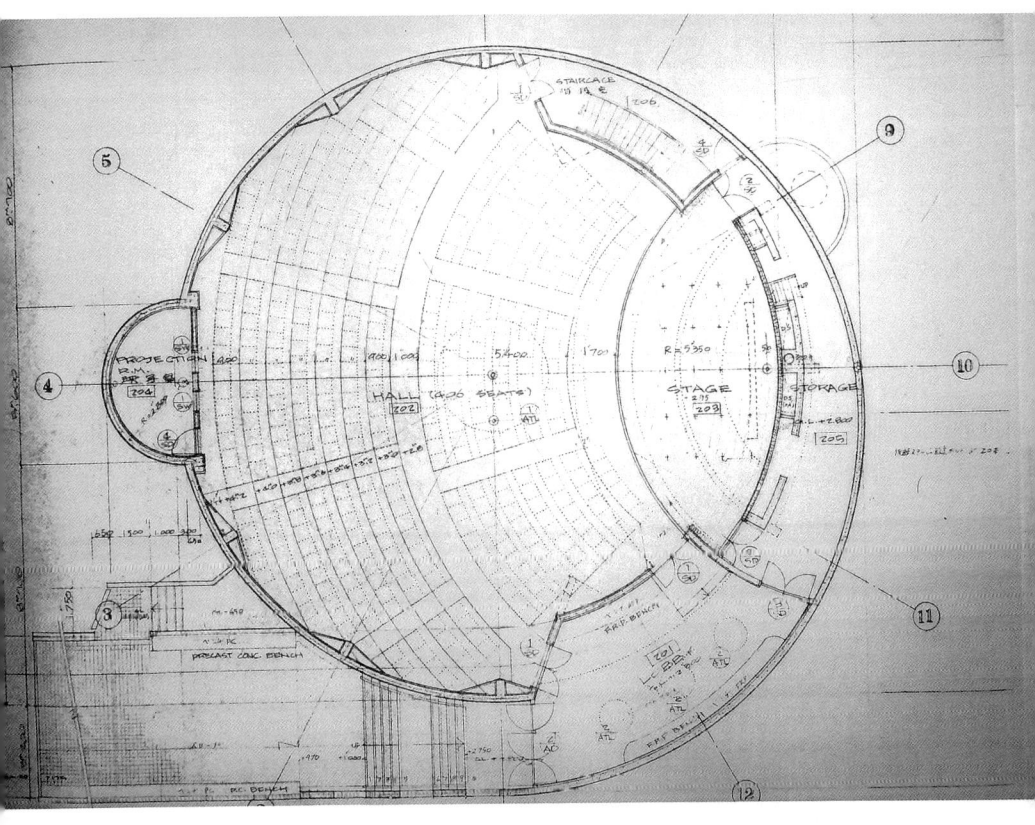

平面図　FloorPlans

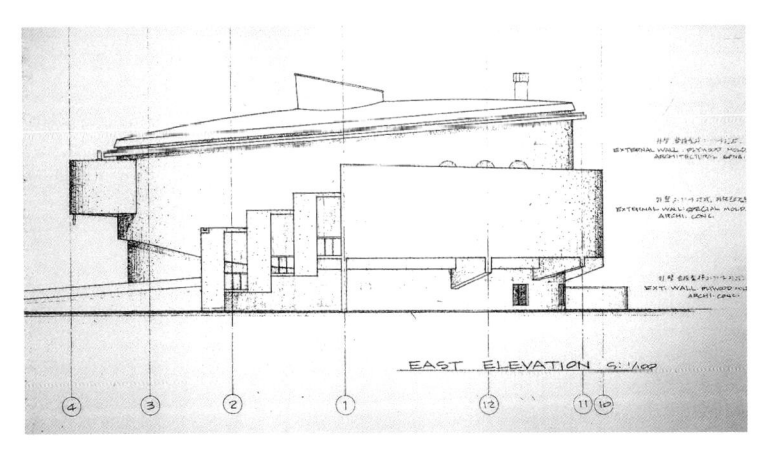

東正面図　East Elevation

▲リズムのあるエントランスキャノピー
◀飛び出したミキサールームの雨落とし　子供たちは水遊びをする。

▲ Rhythmic entrance canopy.
◀ A rainwater drain pipe protrudes from the audio mixing room: Kids play with the water.

▲エントランスよりアプローチを見る。

Entrance view from the front door.

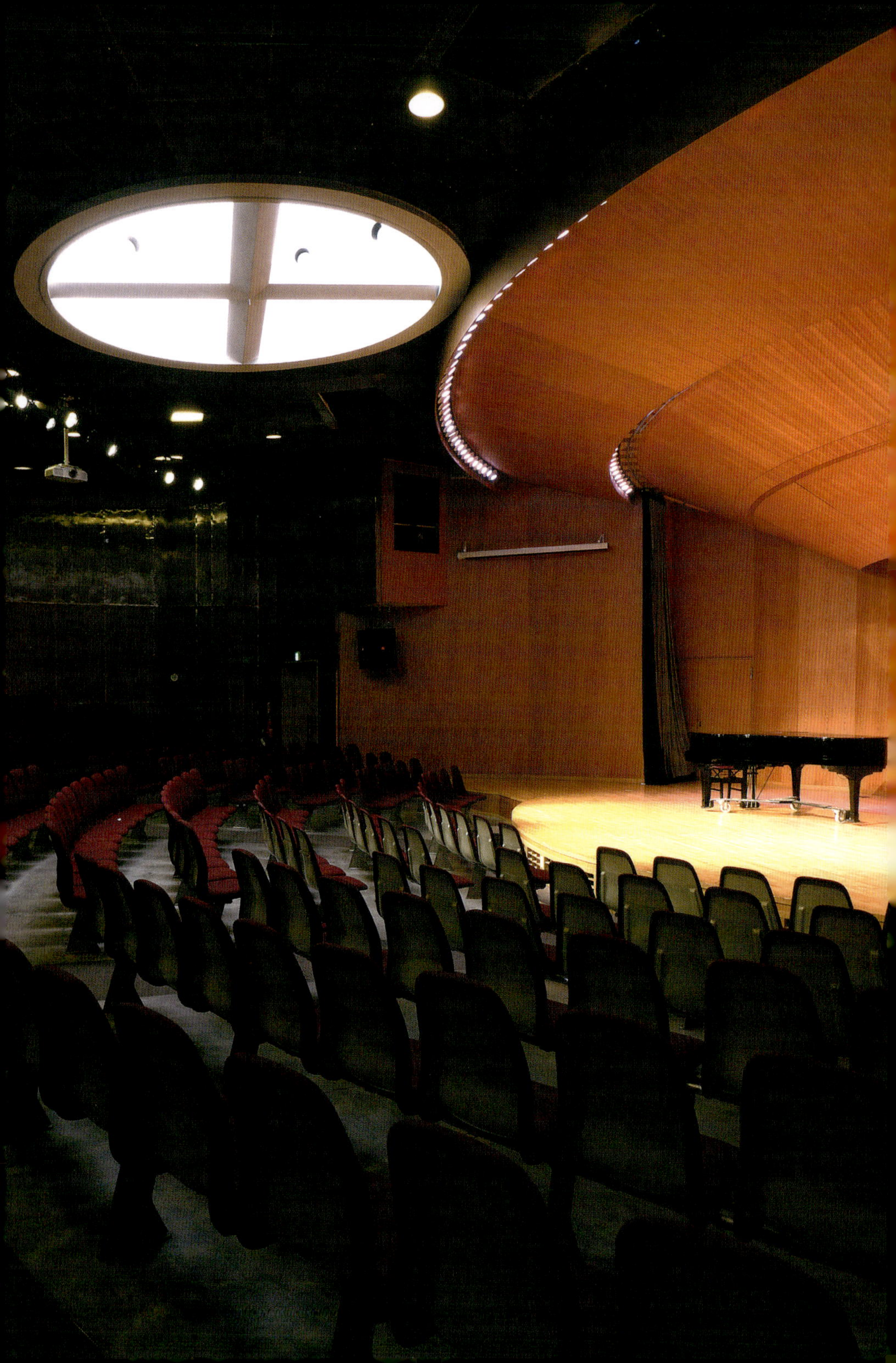

◀200席ほどの小ホールに十字架のトップライトからの光がこぼれる。
▼ステージ側から見ると包まれるような感じがする円形ホールと十字架。

◀ In a small hall with about 200 seats, light showers from the sky light with a cross.
▼ From the stage side, the round hall and cross make one feel enclosed.

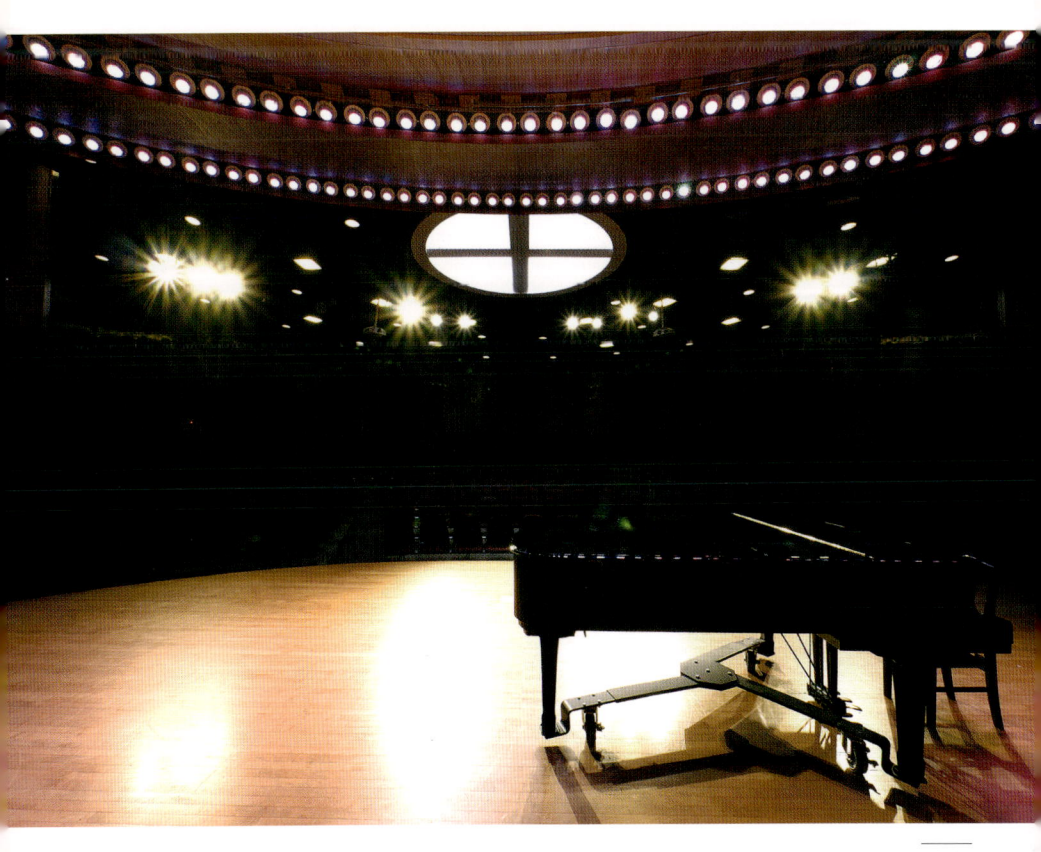

「建築家は60歳になって一人前！」と彼はいった。
土屋重文

代表作品の年譜からの考察

　A・レーモンドさんの作品年譜は第二次世界大戦をはさんで前期、後期の大きく二つに分けることができる。

　前期は、フランク・L・ライトの元から独立した32歳から第二次世界大戦前の50歳までである。前期の前半は、ライトの呪縛が強く、ライト調が色濃くのこる作品が多い。例えば、東京女子大学（1921年 33歳）、聖路加病院（1928年 40歳）、トレッドソン別邸（1930年 42歳）である。東京女子大学のチャペル（1943年 46歳）は、キャンパス計画の10数年後であったこともあり、A・ペレーのランシーの教会からヒントを得て、ライト色を消そうとしている。

　前期の後半はライト色を消すために、たびたび、コルビュジエのデザイン力を借りている。年齢はコルビュジエが1歳年上であることから、親近感とライバル意識を同時に感じていたのではないだろうかと私は思っている。

　その例が、霊南坂の家（1923年 35歳）、軽井沢夏の家（1933年 45歳）、ニューホープの家（1939年 51歳）である。

　軽井沢の聖パウロ教会（1934年 46歳）は、大学までをチェコで過ごした時の田舎にあった教会の原風景からのインスピレーションであると思う。イタリー大使別邸（1928年 40歳）、スタンダード石油社宅（1928年 40歳）などからはオリジナリティーが明らかに感じとれるようになる。

　60歳からの後期は、終戦後の1948年の再来日から、1973年 85歳でアメリカへ戻るまでで、まさしく「60歳で一人前…」を実証するが如く、再来日の年から次々と代表作を発表していく。おそらく、戦争中の10年間に温めていたものが、一気に大噴火したのではないかと思えるほどである。再来日の年のリーダースダイジェスト支社（1949年 61歳　日本建築学会賞）、その翌年1950年の自邸＋レーモンド事務所。

　そして、次のように続く。
・1951年（63歳）銀座ヤマハビル＋ホール、御木本真珠日本橋店
・1952年（64歳）アメリカ大使館アパート、サロモン邸

東京女子大学チャペル・1934年

Chapel in Tokyo Woman's Christian University, 1934.

軽井沢夏の家・1933年

Summer House, Karuizawa, 1933.

チェコの木造教会　15世紀

St. Francis of Assisi Church in the Czech Republic. 15th century.

He said, "An architect is full-fledged when he is 60."
Shigefumi Tsuchiya

Discussion Based on a Chronological List of his Representative Works

The chronological list of works of Mr. Antonin Raymond can be roughly divided into early and late periods before and after World War II.

The early period is from when he became independent from Frank Lloyd Wright at the age of 32, to age 50 before World War II began. The first half of the early period was still under the strong spell of Wright, and his works were largely influenced by Wright. Such examples are Tokyo Woman's Christian University (1921, 33 years old), St. Luke's International Hospital (1928, 40 years old), and Troedsson Villa (1930, 42 years old). The Chapel in Tokyo Woman's Christian University (1943, 46 years old) was designed more than ten years later than the campus plan. He was inspired by Auguste Perret's Notre Dame du Raincy and tried to erase Wright's influence.

In the second half of his early period, he often borrowed the design skills of Le Corbusier, in order to delete Wright's influence. Since Le Corbusier was one year older, I think Mr. Raymond might have felt an affinity and a rivalry at the same time.

Such examples include Reinanzaka House (1923, 35 years old), Summer House, Karuizawa (1933, 45 years old), and Raymond Farm, New Hope (1939, 51 years old).

I think the St. Paul's Catholic Church in Karuizawa (1934, 46 years old) was inspired by a primal scene of a church in rural Czech Republic, where he lived until college. His originality can be clearly seen in the Italian Embassy Nikko Villa (1928, 40 years old) and Standard Oil Co. Housing (1928, 40 years old).

His latter period started in 1948, when he was 60 and re-visiting Japan after the war, and it ended in 1986, when he was 85 and went back to the U.S. As if to prove the "full-fledged when he is 60...." dictum, he consecutively published representative works starting from the year when he returned to Japan.

It seems like the ideas that had been simmering during the ten years of the war erupted all at once. In the year of his return, the Reader's Digest

- 1953年（65歳）安川電機本社ビル、カニンガム邸
- 1954年（66歳）聖アンセルモ目黒教会、森村邸
- 1955年（67歳）聖アルバン教会、聖パトリック教会
- 1957年（69歳）葉山別荘、延岡ルーテル教会
- 1958年（70歳）群馬音楽センター、伊藤邸
- 1959年（71歳）イラン大使館、ICU図書館
- 1961年（73歳）聖ミカエル教会、聖ポール教会、立教高校
- 1962年（74歳）軽井沢の新スタジオ、南山大学、東京ゴルフクラブ
- 1963年（75歳）松坂屋銀座店、神言会修道院
- 1964年（76歳）神言神学院＋チャペル
- 1965年（77歳）新発田カトリック教会、サンカロス大学キャンパス計画
- 1966年（78歳）足立邸、カナディアン・アカデミー
- 1967年（79歳）岡山大学体育館、インド宗教センター計画
- 1968年（80歳）上智大学6，7号館、イスラエル大使館
- 1969年（81歳）ハワイ大キャンパス計画
- 1970年（82歳）高崎哲学堂計画、クリスチャン・アカデミー音楽堂
- 1971年（83歳）マースクライン横浜支社、旧韓国大使館

レーモンド事務所風景

Scenes in the Raymond Office.

レーモンド哲学5原則とレーモンドスタイル

戦後の再来日の翌年1950年（62歳）に発表したレーモンド自邸＋事務所は、たいへん画期的な建築である。

　この建築には、レーモンド哲学5原則である「単純、自然、直截、機能的、経済的かつ心から創ること」のすべてが守られている。ここから後に言われる「レーモンドスタイル」が生まれ、発展していくことになる。

　この建築は、今でよく言われる「ローコスト・エコ建築」である。木造建築の新しい試みは、建築家や構造設計者や建築会社などからさまざまになされているが、60年経ったいまでもこれを超える建築が出てきていないと考える。

　すべての主要な架構材は、80〜100∅の丸太材である。前の年に竣工したリーダースダイジェスト支社の足場に使用した後の廃材になった丸太をもらい受け、磨きもせずにそのまま使用した。大工手間を節約するために、ジョイント部はすべてボル

Offices (1949, 61 years old, awarded the Prize of Architectural Institute of Japan) were designed, followed by the Raymond House and Studio a year later, in 1950. Then his works continued as follows:
- 1951 (63 years old) Ginza Yamaha Building and Hall, Mikimoto Pearl Shop in Nihonbashi
- 1952 (64 years old) U.S. Embassy Apartment, Salomon House
- 1953 (65 years old) Head Office of Yasukawa Electric Corporation, Cunningham House
- 1954 (66 years old) St. Anselm's Church, Morimura House
- 1955 (67 years old) St. Alban's Church, St. Patrick's Catholic Church
- 1957 (69 years old) Hayama Villa, the Lutheran Church in Nobeoka
- 1958 (70 years old) Gunma Music Center, Ito House
- 1959 (71 years old) Embassy of Iran, ICU Library
- 1961 (73 years old) St. Michael's Anglican Episcopal Church, St. Paul's Catholic Church, Rikkyo High School
- 1962 (74 years old) New Studio, Karuizawa, Nanzan University Tokyo Golf Club
- 1963 (75 years old) Matsuzakaya Ginza Shop, Divine Word Seminary in Tokyo
- 1964 (76 years old) Divine Word Seminary Chapel in Nagoya
- 1965 (77 years old) Shibata Catholic Church, Campus Plan of University of San Calros
- 1966 (78 years old) Adachi House, Canadian Academy
- 1967 (79 years old) Okayama University Gymnasium, Plan of India Religion Center
- 1968 (80 years old) Sophia University No. 6 and 7 buildings, Embassy of Israel
- 1969 (81 years old) Campus Plan of University of Hawaii
- 1970 (82 years old) Plan of Takasaki Philosophical Building, Christian Academy Concert Hall
- 1971 (83 years old) Maersk Line Building in Yokohama, Former Embassy of Korea

Five Principles of the Raymond Philosophy and Style

Raymond House and Studio, which was revealed in 1950, a year after his return to Japan (62 years old), is a significantly innovative architectural work.

In this architecture, all of the five principles of the Raymond

ト一本だけのジョイントである。ホゾ加工、補強金物は一切使っていない。

　建具の障子、襖は不整形の丸太柱の難しい取り合いさけるため、柱の外側へ建具位置をずらしている。これは、住宅でのカーテンウォール工法のはしりである。屋根は安価で軽量にするため、カラー鉄板瓦棒葺きである。内部の天井は貼らずに、野地板を現したままであった。野地板現し天井には、布巻き電線と丸いガイシが有機的な味付けをしていた。

　壁はすべて3mmのロータリーベニヤ仕上げ、床は2mmの薄いプラスチックタイルといった最低の仕上げである。麻布時代の30年間は、台風や地震にもまったく問題なく耐えられた。一本のボルトジョイントのため、全ジョイント部で台風圧や地震力からしなやかに力を吸収している。

　この建築の最も秀逸なことは、空間である。この空間に身をおくと、丸太の柱とシザー・トラス（挟み梁工法）が心地良い緊張感をもたらし、アクセントになっている。空間全体と細部まで美しいプロポーション、すべての適切な素材に障子越しに射し込む柔らかい外光がとても心地よく優しく包みこんでくれる。

　レーモンドさんはよくこんなことを言っていた。
「大きなプロジェクトを手がける時は、同時並行で住宅の設計をやりなさい！そうしないとスケールのバランス感覚が狂ってしまう。」

　このことを実証するようにオールマイティーの建築家としては珍しいくらいの夥しい数、おそらく120軒ちかく、計画を入れると200軒以上の住宅を設計している。

　レーモンドさんは最晩年の85歳、病のためアメリカに帰る決心をした。アメリカでの住まいはニューホープにある大きな家ではなく、ノエミ夫人と余生を過ごすために新たに小住宅の設計をして、亡くなる88歳までの3年間をそこで過ごしている。あの永年のライバルであったコルビュジェのカップマルタンの家を思い浮かべてしまう。

晩年のライフスタイル

朝天気が良いと、レーモンドさんはノエミ夫人と二匹の愛犬を連れて近くをよく散歩していた。帰ってくると、冬と雨の日以

レーモンド自邸居間・1950年
1978年代々木レーモンド設計事務所ビルに移築時の写真

Living room in Raymond's house, 1950.

philosophy are fulfilled: simple, natural, straightforward, functional, and economical but created from the heart. From these, what came to be known later as the "Raymond Style" was born and developed.

This architecture is currently often called a "low cost eco-house". Although various new trials for wooden buildings have been conducted by architects, structural designers, or builders, an architectural work that exceeds this has not yet appeared after 60 years.

All of the main frame materials are round timbers with 80 to 100 mm diameter. We were given waste round timbers, which were used for scaffolding for the construction of the Reader's Digest Offices (completed in the previous year), and used them without sanding. In order to minimize the carpenters' work, all of the joints were connected with only one bolt. Mortise joints or reinforcing metal were not used.

In order to avoid the difficult details of uneven shaped round timber pillars, sliding screens and sliding doors were shifted to the outside of the pillars. This was the beginning of the curtain wall method in houses. Ribbed seam roofing with colored steel sheets was used in order to reduce the cost and weight. For the interior, the ceiling was not covered and roof boards were exposed. Cloth-wrapped electric cords and round insulators added an organic flavor to the exposed roof boards.

It was made with minimum finish; for example, all walls were finished with rotary-cut veneers of 3mm thickness and floors were 2mm thin plastic tile. For 30 years in Azabu, it survived through typhoons and earthquakes without any problem. Since the house used the single bolt joints, all of the joints flexibly absorbed stresses from typhoons and earthquakes.

The most brilliant part of this architectural work is its space. In this space, round timber pillars and scissor trusses (tucked beam method) provided a comfortable unease, and also added an accent. The entire space, the beautiful proportion down to the smallest details, all of the proper materials used, and soft sunlight through sliding screens all comfortably and softly surrounded us.

Mr. Raymond often said, "When working on a large-scale project, design a house simultaneously! Otherwise, you will lose a sense of balance."

As if to prove this, he designed almost 120 houses, or more than 200 houses including plans. Such a large number was rare for an almighty architect.

Mr. Raymond decided to go back to the U.S. in his later years, at 85 years old, due to illness. In the U.S., he did not live in a big house in

外は、きれいな庭の見える藤棚付のパティオで朝食をとるのが日課であった。
　我々が出勤するころには、自分のスタジオ内で仕事を始めている。午前と午後に一回ずつ、スタッフ全員のところを一巡して回り、指示をだしたり、時にはスタッフの席に座ってアドバイスや修正のスケッチをしてくれる。
　午後の三時になると欧米式のティータイムがある。時間のある時はレーモンドさんも参加して、建築談議に花が咲くこともあった。この時間は実に新鮮で楽しいひと時であった。それ以外の時間は、図面を書くエンピツの音や歩く靴の音ぐらいで、静まりかえっている。初めの頃は自分の前の電話がなるとビックリして心臓が止まる思いであった。
　ふと気づくと、朝晩で服装を着替えて楽しまれていることが時々あった。決して贅沢な服を着るわけではなく、時にはネクタイに大きなシミをつけていたりもした。私が2，3日も同じネクタイで仕事をしていると、気遣ってか使い古しの自分のネクタイを譲ってくれた。今もその一本は宝物としてオフィスに大切に保管している。
　残業で夜遅くまで残っていると、時々であるがチェロやピアノの心地良い音がもれてくる。時には、鼻唄まじりでブランディー片手にニコニコ顔で現われることもあった。静かな時は、かならず絵を描いたり、仕事をしたり、読書をしていた。とにかく、毎日毎日が楽しくてしょうがないといった気持ちが伝わってきて、羨ましく思えた。こんなライフスタイルが、その後の私の目標となった。
　麻布の丸太造りの建物はローコストで、夏は暑く、冬は寒い。レーモンドさんはチェコ出身なので、冬は平気であった。真夏の日でクーラーの効きの悪い時は、悲鳴をあげてアトリエからよく飛び出してくることがあった。そんな時は庭に行き、屋根にホースで水をたっぷりかけたことは実に楽しい思い出になっている。

ノエミさんと恐妻家レーモンドさん

　先輩からレーモンドさんは「気難しく、頑固で、厳しく、すぐに怒りだす。」と聞いていた。入社一年目の頃は、レーモンドさんの前だと、過度の緊張でまともな会話もできなかったが、

レーモンド自邸の中庭　ここでレーモンド夫妻はよく食事をとった。

Central courtyard in Raymond's house: Mr. and Mrs. Raymond often had meals here.

New Hope. Instead, he newly designed a small house to spend his last years with his wife, Noémi, and lived three more years until he died at age 88. This reminds me of his long-time rival Le Corbusier's house in Cap-Martin.

Lifestyle in His Later Years

When the weather was fine in the morning, Mr. Raymond and his wife, Noémi, often took their two beloved dogs for a walk around the neighborhood. Except during winter and rainy days, after a walk they usually had breakfast on the patio where a wisteria trellis stood and a view of the beautiful garden could be enjoyed.

By the time we went to the office, he was working in his studio. Once in the morning and once in the afternoon, he came to all of the staff members and gave directions. Sometimes, he sat in the staff member's seat, gave advice, or fixed their sketches.

At 3 o'clock, a European-style teatime was held. When Mr Raymond had time he would join us, and sometimes discussions about architecture became quite animated. This teatime was really fresh and fun. The rest of the time was quiet except for the sound of pencils drawing or someone walking. When I was new, I was so surprised by the ringing of the phone that I thought my heart would stop.

I noticed that he sometimes enjoyed a different outfit in the morning and afternoon. They were never luxurious, and there was occasionally a big stain on his necktie. When I wore the same necktie for several days, out of possible concern he gave me one of his old ones. That necktie is my treasure and it is still carefully stored at my office.

When I worked late at night, soothing cello or piano music was played once in a while. At times, he appeared humming and smiling with a glass of brandy in one hand. When he was quiet, he was always painting, working, or reading. This lifestyle became my goal later on.

The building in Azabu was made with logs and for a low cost. It was hot in summer and cold in winter.

Mr. Raymond was from the Czech Republic and he could take the coldness in winter. But when the air conditioning did not work well in summer, he often cried out and ran out of his studio. It is a fun memory that we went out to the garden in such times and sprayed plenty of water on the roof with a hose.

私には優しかった。入社時、レーモンドさんは82歳、私は22歳であるから孫扱いされたのではないかと思う。

　私がスランプになって暗い表情になっていたりすると、私の傍にきて耳元で「今日は天気が良いので庭の芝生をかってくれないかと？」といって、午前中から気分転換をさせてくれたこともあった。ある時は、「ノエミがプールで泳ぎたがっているので、プール掃除をしてくれないか？」と頼まれた。午前中から水着でプール掃除をしているうちに、落ち込んだ気分がすっかりと晴れていった。

　ある朝、ノエミ夫人が居間からスタッフルームに「プールでおぼれているので助けてください。」と大声で叫びながら入ってきた。ビックリして、私が庭のプールに駆けつけてみると誰もおぼれていない。ノエミさんが「よく見なさい！」というので、目をこらしてみてビックリした。何と、食べ過ぎのガマガエルがバタバタしながら沈んでいくところだった。すぐに、昆虫採取用ネットですくい上げて一件落着した楽しい大騒動があった。当時、ノエミさんは日本の動物愛護協会の副会長を務めていた。

　「レーモンド展」準備の慰労もあった軽井沢の新スタジオへ連れて行かれた時のこと。夕食はバーベキューになり、皆が席についた。すぐに大きな体のレーモンドさんの腕に蚊が何匹かとまったが、決して叩かず、さされるままにしている。

　ずいぶんと我慢強いのか、鈍いのかと失礼なことを考えていた時、ノエミ夫人が席をたった。夫人が見えなくなると、あわてて蚊を叩き始めた。ビックリして見ていると、レーモンドさんが口に人差し指をあて、「シー」という内緒のサインを出したので、思わず吹き出しそうになったこともあった。

ノエミさん設計のストゥール　家具のデザインはほとんどがノエミさん

Stools designed by Noémi: Most of the furniture was designed by Noémi.

ノエミさん設計の椅子

Chair designed by Noémi.

眼を真っ赤にしたレーモンドさん

私が入所したのは1970年で、10～12色のカラーペンが世に出始めた頃である。事務所のスタッフはまだ誰も使っていなかった。私は学校の延長で、スケッチにカラーペンを使っていた。それをレーモンドさんは見つけ、カラーペンのセットを貸してくれといって、アトリエに持っていき、その日はアトリエから出てこなかった。

　翌朝、ニコニコしながら私のところに来て、昨日ペンを全部

Noémi and her Submissive Husband, Mr. Raymond

My predecessors told me that Mr. Raymond was "difficult, stubborn, strict, and bad-tempered." For the first year of work, I was so nervous in front of Mr. Raymond and barely had normal conversations. But he was nice to me. At that time, Mr. Raymond was 82 years old and I was 22, so I think he treated me like his grandson.

When I fell into a slump and had a dark expression, he came and said in my ear, "Today is such a fine day. I wondered if you could mow the lawn." That was how he would let me refresh in the morning. Another time, he said, "Noémi wants to swim in the pool. Would you please clean the pool?" As I wore my swimsuit and cleaned the pool in the morning, my depression went away completely.

One morning, Noémi stormed into the staffroom from the living room, loudly shouting, "Please help, he's drowning in the pool!"

I was surprised and rushed to the pool in the garden but nobody was drowning. Noémi said, "Look carefully!", so I did and was surprised. A toad, having obviously eaten too much, was thrashing and drowning. I immediately scooped it out with an insect net and everything went well. It was a fun incident. At that time, Noémi was famous for her love of animals, and she was a vice president of the Japanese Humane Society.

Once he took us to the New Studio in Karuizawa, and this trip was a thank-you gift for preparing the "Raymond Exhibition". We barbequed for dinner and everyone was seated. Soon, several mosquitos flew onto the arm of Mr. Raymond, who was a large man, but he did not kill them and just let them bite.

I was in the middle of rudely wondering whether he was extremely patient or just dull, when Noémi left the table. As soon as his wife went out of sight, he rushed to squash the mosquitos. I was astonished and watched him. Then I almost burst out in laughter because Mr. Raymond put his finger to his lips and said "Shh", signaling me to keep it secret.

Red-eyed Mr. Raymond

I started working at the office in 1970, when ten to twelve colored pens appeared on the market. None of the office staff members used them. I

使ってしまったので、もう3セット買ってきてほしいと頼まれた。昨夜一日だけで使い切ってしまうとは、そうとうのスケッチをしたのだろうと思いつつ、購入して3セット手渡しした。

それから2, 3日後の朝、目を真っ赤にしたレーモンドさんは、私をこっそりとアトリエに呼んでくれた。目の前に80号の絵が2枚掲げてあり、私は言葉を失ってしまった。2枚の絵はあのカラーペンで、しかも全面点描画で描きあげてあった。

昼間は通常に設計の仕事をしていて夕方から描き始め、一週間足らずで2枚の点描画を仕上げたことになる。おそらく一日、二日は徹夜したはずである。この時、レーモンドさんは82歳！ どこからこの尋常ではないエネルギーが出てくるのであろうか。レーモンドさんの仕事は当時現役のバリバリでクリスチャン・アカデミー音楽堂、韓国大使館、マースクラインビル等々を手がけていた。私はその時22歳で、体力的には絶対の自信があったので、レーモンドさんにはどこまでも付いていこうと決心をしたことを、懐かしく思い出す。

今、その絵はレーモンド事務所のロビーにかけられている。

レーモンドさんがカラーペンで描いた80号の画

No. 80 size picture drawn by Mr. Raymond with colored pens.

「地球人」レーモンドさんのこと

私の父は、子供の頃に父親を亡くした。丁稚奉公をしながらの苦学の連続で大学までぐでた。必要にせまられ経済学を専攻したそうである。高校に入学したころに、これからは英会話を身に着けないとダメだと考えたが、英会話教室に通うお金もないので英国人の元でのアルバイトを探した。新聞にのっていた先が、陶芸家のイギリス人バーナード・リーチである。仕事は手回し轆轤をまわすもので、作業をしながら英会話を一年ほど習った。それは1919年、大正8年のことである。

リーチが帰英するときに、英会話の勉強をさらに続けたいので、良い人を紹介してほしいと懇願した。紹介されたのは、A・レーモンドさんである。私はこの話を聞いて、奇縁だなと思った。父はレーモンド設計で事務のアルバイトをしながらレーモンドさんから直接英会話を学ぶことになる。後に父から聞いた話は「地球人」レーモンドさんを感じるエピソードであった。

父は昼間レーモンド事務所で働き、夜は日大の夜学で経済学を専攻した。その後、定年まで日大で教鞭をとることになる。

1934年、父は経済学を実践で身につけようと考え、当時、

used them for sketching as I did in school.

Mr. Raymond found these and asked to borrow them. He took them to his studio and never came out that day.

The following morning, he came to me smiling and asked me to get three more sets because he used up mine the day before. I immediately bought three sets and handed them to him, while thinking that he must have done a lot of sketches to use them up in one day.

A few days later, a red-eyed Mr. Raymond secretly called me to his studio. Two No. 80 size paintings hung in front of me, and I was at a loss for words. The two pictures were done with the colored pens, and furthermore, the entirety of each picture was done in a pointillist manner.

He worked as usual during the daytime, started drawing in the evening, and finished two pointillistic pictures in less than a week. He probably stayed up all night for a day or two. Mr. Raymond was 82 years old at this time! Where did he get this extraordinary energy? At that time I was age 22 and had absolute confidence in my stamina. I remember with nostalgia that I decided to follow Mr. Raymond forever.

The pictures are currently in the lobby of the Raymond Office.

"Earthman" Mr. Raymond

My father lost his father in his youth. He served his apprenticeship and worked his way through college. His major was economics out of necessity. When he entered high school, he felt a need to acquire English conversation skills for the future, and he looked for a part time job under English speakers since he did not have money for English lessons. One listed in the newspaper was for the English potter, Bernard Leach. His job was to manually rotate a potter's wheel, and he learned English during his work for about a year, in 1919.

When Leach went back to the UK, my father begged him to introduce someone in order to continue learning English, and Mr. Raymond became that new teacher. I felt a strange coincidence when I heard this. My father did office work at the Raymond Architectural Design Office and learned English directly from Mr. Raymond. Later, I heard a story from my father, and it was an episode that depicted "Earthman" Mr. Raymond.

My father worked at the Raymond Office during the daytime, and went to night school at Nihon University where he majored in economics. Later on, he taught at Nihon University until his

渋谷道玄坂にあったフルーツパーラー『マスミ』へ行き、店を売ってくれないかと交渉した。当時、人脈のない父には、先方と折り合った金額の金の工面先がなかった。考えあぐねた末、レーモンドさんに頼みこむことになる。

　しばらくしてレーモンドさんがその大金を用立てしてくれた。父は商売にも精をだし、何年かして用立てしてくれた全額を返しきった。その席でレーモンドさんは「あの時は僕も金がなく、友人、知人から借りて集めた。」と驚愕の話をしたそうである。父は男泣きをし、「命の恩人」のように感じ、生涯レーモンドさんの元で勤めあげる決心をする。1921年から1973年の52年間、レーモンドさんがアメリカに帰るまで父は顧問として経理の面を見ることになった。

　レーモンドさんの秘書に葵文(チェムン)さんがいた。葵さんは1960年代の韓国の学生運動のリーダーであった。命が危ない状況になり、妻と離婚をして、漁船に乗り込んで日本に密入国した。

　密航後は身を潜めながら、友人の助けを借りたり、日本の朝鮮人学校などでアルバイトをして最低限の生活をおくっていた。ある日、英字新聞にレーモンドさんが「コックを求む！」の広告をだす。それを見つけた葵さんは、料理などにまったく自信はなかったが、即刻、レーモンド事務所に駆けつけた。何とか、住み込みの形で潜りこむことに成功する。

　葵さんの頭の良さに気づいたレーモンドさんは、自分の秘書にならないかと声をかけた。身元保証人にレーモンドさんがなって、葵さんは日本の国籍をとることになる。レーモンドさんを「命の恩人」であると常々いっていた葵さんは、レーモンドさんが死ぬまで身の周りの世話をすると公言していた。レーモンドさんがアメリカに帰国する際に同行し、1976年、レーモンドさんを看取るまで仕えた。その後、自分のしたかったレストランをアメリカで開いたと連絡があった。

日本の近代建築の父と「地球人」

レーモンドさんは88年の生涯で、半生の43年間もの長きを日本で過ごした。「日本の近代建築の父」でもあったその「レーモンドスクール」の卒業生は、前川國男、吉村順三、増沢洵、ジョージ中島等をはじめ数えきれない。それは正しく、日本の近代建築の大事な礎を築いたといえる。なにゆえか、吉田松陰の

retirement.

In 1934, he decided to acquire economic knowledge through practical activities. He went to the fruit parlor "Masumi", which was located in Dogenzaka, Shibuya back in those days, and negotiated to buy the shop. At that point, he did not have personal connections to raise the negotiated amount of money. After thinking hard about it, he asked for it from Mr. Raymond.

After a while, Mr. Raymond prepared the large amount of money. My father worked hard and returned all of the money after a few years. When he did so, Mr. Raymond told an astonishing story: "At the time, I also had no money, so I borrowed it from my friends and acquaintances." My father wept and felt that Mr. Raymond was his "lifesaver". He decided to work for Mr. Raymond for life. For 52 years from 1921 to 1973, until Mr. Raymond returned to the U.S., my father was in charge of accounting as his advisor.

Bun Aoi was Mr. Raymond's secretary. He was a student movement leader in Korea in the 1960s. His life became threatened if he got caught, so he divorced his wife and smuggled himself into Japan on a fishing boat.

After arriving, he hid and had a minimal life by receiving support from his friends or working part time in a Korean school in Japan. One day, Mr. Raymond posted an advertisement for "Cook needed!" in an English newspaper. Mr. Aoi found it and immediately ran to the Raymond Office, though he had no confidence in his cooking. He managed to get a live-in position.

Mr. Raymond recognized Mr. Aoi's intelligence, and asked Mr. Aoi to be his secretary. Mr. Aoi received Japanese nationality by Mr. Raymond providing a personal reference. Mr. Aoi always said Mr. Raymond was his "lifesaver", and he professed that he would take care of Mr. Raymond until the end. He went to the U.S. when Mr. Raymond returned there, and served Mr. Raymond until he died in 1976. Later on, I heard that he opened a restaurant in the U.S., which was his dream.

Father of Japanese Modern Architecture

In the 88 years of Mr. Raymond's life, he stayed in Japan for half of it, a long 43 years. The numerous graduates of the "Raymond School", which was the "father of Japanese modern architecture", include Kunio Maekawa, Junzo Yoshimura, Makoto Masuzawa, George Nakashima,

「松下村塾」とダブって見えてしまう。

　レーモンドさんはユダヤ人である。チェコのプラハ工科大学を出たが、欧州では仕事が少なく1910年にアメリカに渡った。家族はその後アウシュビッツ収容所で全員虐殺される。この悲惨な過去の記憶があるために戦後のチェコには一度も帰ることができなかった。

　それから察すると、学生までの22年間住んだチェコ人でもなく、国籍はアメリカであったが通算して23年間暮らしたアメリカ人でもなく、43年の長きにわたって過ごした日本人でもなかった。ジプシーのように祖国を失い、そのアイデンティティーの喪失の空洞を埋めようとおそらく意識はせずに夢中で建築、絵画、音楽、そして戦前の日本文化を探求したのではないか。それは、正しく、禅僧のようなストイックで気の遠くなるほどの長い孤高の戦いであったと思える。そこに触れないと、あの寛大で慈愛に満ちた行動を理解することはできない。

　私の接した最晩年のレーモンドさんは、私から見て「地球人レーモンド」になることによって、失ったアイデンティティーを取り戻したように思える。そのアイデンティティーを取り戻そうと足掻いていた頃、フランク・ロイド・ライトの助手として1919年、31歳で念願の日本に来ることができた。

　西洋文化に侵されていない戦前の日本の町並みと民家の美しさに魅了される。そして、日本人の慎ましい生活、武士道の心を感じる人間性に触れ、安住の地を見つけた感をもったと思う。数年であるが、目黒辺りの民家でも生活している。

　レーモンドさんは建築家に一番必要で大事なことは哲学的思考がベースにあることだと強調していた。前川國男、白井晟一もまったく同じことを言っていたのを思い出す。

　それが「建築家は60歳になってはじめて一人前…！」につながる。根拠のない流行に振り回されず、焦らず、一途に追い求め続けることである。建築を仕事と捉えるのでなく、絵や音楽にむかうようにライフワーク的に考えると人生の正しい道筋が自然と見えてくる。

ライトとレーモンド　旧帝国ホテル工事中の現場にて、1921年頃。

Wright and Raymond: At the former Imperial Hotel construction site, around 1921.

etc. It surely established the important foundation of Japanese modern architecture. For some reason, it seems to overlap with Shoka Sonjuku by Shoin Yoshida.

Mr. Raymond was Jewish. He graduated from the Czech Technical University in Prague. However, there was only a few jobs in Europe and he moved to the U.S. in 1910. Later, all of his family members were slaughtered in the Auschwitz concentration camp. Due to this tragic memory, he was never able to go back to Czechoslovakia after the war.

Considering this, he was not Czech, though he lived there for 22 years until he finished school; he was not American, though his nationality was American and he lived there for a total of 23 years; and he was not Japanese, though he lived there for 43 years. He lost his mother country as if he were a gypsy. It is probable that he intently explored architecture, arts, music, and pre-war Japanese culture, in the course of his attempts to fill the emptiness due to his lost identity, although he was not aware of it. It must have been a Zen monk-like stoic, immeasurably long and lonely fight. Without knowing this, his generous behavior filled with affection cannot be understood.

The Mr. Raymond that I knew in his later years seemed to me to have retrieved his identity, which was once lost, by becoming "Earthman Mr. Raymond". During his time of struggle for an identity, his long-cherished dream was realized and he came to Japan as an assistant of Frank Lloyd Wright in 1919 when he was 31 years old.

He was fascinated by the beauty of pre-war townscapes and houses in Japan, which were not influenced by European culture. Furthermore, he might have felt that a safe refuge was found through knowing the modest life of the Japanese and their humanity that contains the spirit of Bushido. He lived in a house near Meguro, though it was only for a few years. Mr. Raymond insisted that the most necessary and important thing for an architect was that philosophical thinking exist as a foundation.

This is connected to his saying: "An architect is full-fledged when he is 60." An architect should be patient and seek with all the person's heart, without being swayed by groundless trends. Rather than taking on architectural design as a job, consider it as a lifework such as painting or music, and then a proper way of life can be spontaneously found.

クリスチャン・アカデミー音楽堂のことども
土屋重文

> ガスタンク！

　私がレーモンド設計事務所（当時の所員は40数名）に入所したのは1970年。その年の10月の初めに松坂屋デパートで開催された「レーモンド展」の実行委員に参加したのがきっかけで、5から6名からなるアトリエ・レーモンドで仕事をすることになった。戦後は「アトリエ・レーモンド」と「株式会社レーモンド設計事務所」ははっきりと分かれていた。

　入所後レーモンドさんの元での一作目が「クリスチャン・アカデミー音楽堂」であった。規模は延べ面積が1000㎡弱、2階建て、円形プランのRC壁式構造。外部はすべて打放しコンクリートで、小規模な建築であった。デザインスタッフは、チーフの北澤興一さんと私の2名。私が参加した時は平面計画のスケッチがほぼできあがっていた。ヴォリューム模型をつくるために私が立面のスケッチを描くことになった。

　平面と断面スケッチをもとに書き始めてみたものの、円形で、窓無しで、打放しコンクリートと形にならない要素ばかりであった。

　一応立面図を起こしたが、案の上、翌朝そのスケッチを見たレーモンドさんが「OH！　NO！　ガスタンク！」といった。それから魔の一週間が始まった。

　レーモンド哲学として不必要な装飾をつける訳にはいかず、どう足掻いても脳内が沸騰しそうになるだけで、何回も書き直したものの変り映えしなかった。次の日も次の日も「ガスタンク！」「ガスタンク！」と一週間ほど毎日続いた。

　トラウマのようなその一言で頭の中が一杯になり、思考停止状態でギブアップしようかと思い始めていたその朝、見かねたのだろう、レーモンドさんが私のところに来て座り、ガスタンクの立面図の上に更のトレペを置いた。濃い目の鉛筆で、少々震えた線、晩年のアールトのスケッチのような線で徐々に描き始めた。私はしばしポカーンと凝視しているだけであった。しばらくして書き上げると、レーモンドさんは黙っていってしまった。スケッチを見て目の前で本物のマジックを見せられた感

レーモンド事務所風景

Scenes in the Raymond Office.

Regarding the Christian Academy Concert Hall

Shigefumi Tsuchiya

Gas Tank!

I became a member of the Raymond Architectural Design Office in 1970 (there were about 40 staff members at that time). I seized this opportunity when I became a planning committee member of the "Raymond Exhibition", which was held in early October in the same year at the Matsuzakaya department store, and I joined the Atelier Raymond that had five or six workers. After the war, the "Atelier Raymond" and "Raymond Architectural Design Office" were clearly separated.

The first project under Mr. Raymond was the "Christian Academy Concert Hall". It had a total floor space of about 1000m3, two stories, and a round plan with a structure of reinforced concrete walls. The building was small and all of the exterior walls were as-cast concrete. The design staff was only two people: the chief, Koichi Kitazawa, and me. When I joined, most of the sketches of the floor plan were completed. In order to make a volume model, I was supposed to draw a sketch of the elevation plan.

I started drawing based on the floor plan and the sectional sketch, but it was full of elements that were non-formable, such as the round plan, lack of windows, and as-cast concrete.

I somehow managed to make an elevation plan, but as I expected, Mr. Raymond saw it the next morning and said, "Oh no, a gas tank!" Then a nightmare week began.

Due to the Raymond philosophy, adding unnecessary decoration was prohibited. Even though I gave my best effort, my brain almost started boiling, and the plan did not make much progress after drawing many revisions. Day after day, I heard "gas tank!", "gas tank!" for almost a week.

My head was full of that traumatic phrase, my brain stopped working, and I was about to give up one morning. That same morning, Mr. Raymond might have felt sorry to see my struggle and came to sit at my desk. He put new tracing paper on the gas tank-like elevation plan. He slowly began drawing with a dark pencil, and his line was a little bit shaky as if from a sketch by Aalto in his later years. I could only stare at it for a while. A little later, Mr. Raymond finished drawing

じで唖然とした。

　これぞ「画竜点睛」ということかと思った。そこには、まったく別の建築が現れていた。ただの「ガスタンク」が一瞬にして「音楽堂」に生まれ変わっていた。

　「巨匠だから」の一言では私自身を納得させられず、その日は一日中落ち込んでしまった。レーモンドさんは、夕方頃に秘書の葵さんと私を、アトリエ兼居間の部屋に呼び出し少し話をした。そして、席を立って戻ってこなかった。目をやると、机の上と床にまでトレペのスケッチが散乱していた。今でも鮮明に目に浮かぶ光景で、膨大な量のスケッチ（ほぼ一週間分）のすべては音楽堂の立面のスケッチであった。私の乏しい語学力を察して、言葉ではなく体感として私に「教え」てくれたのではないかと、だいぶ後になって判った。

　「82歳の私が、一週間経ってやっと良い案・デザインができた。貴方は、まだ、22歳でスタートしたばかりなのだから、できなくて当り前。焦らずにじっくり腰をすえて仕事に取りくみなさい！」と…。

　この事は、その後の私の40年間で、難題にぶつかるたびに、それを乗り越えるエネルギーが湧き上がり必ず解決してくれる源になった。私にとってレーモンドさんが「命の恩人」ともいえる「人生の師」になった瞬間であった。

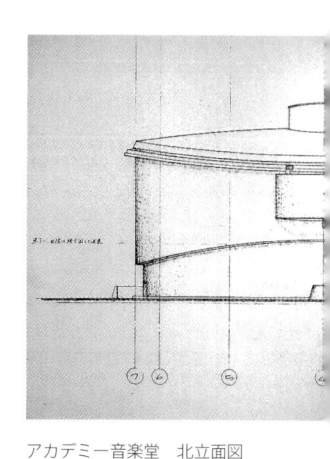

アカデミー音楽堂　北立面図
Academy concert hall floor plan.

妥協してはダメだ！

　一時は建築を諦めようかと思う破目になった立面図がまとまった頃の話。吉村順三さんがレーモンドさんのところに遊びに来た。帰りがけに、書き上げたばかりの立面図を覗き込んですぐに、「君、こっちの方が良いだろう。」と赤ペンを入れながら私にいった。円形プランの真ん中に直径4mのトップライトの勾配が、屋根勾配と逆の方がベターだということだった。

　「レーモンドさん、どう思います？」と吉村さん。しばらくして、「土屋君、吉村君の案が良いと思うので変更しようじゃないか！」一瞬にしてトップライトの角度が逆になった。

　落ちついて眺めて見ると、たしかに良く見えてきた。ちょっと悔しい思い出であるが、「流石だなー！」と今思うと懐かしく楽しい出来事である。

　やっとの思いで実施設計が完了する頃、チーフの北澤興一さ

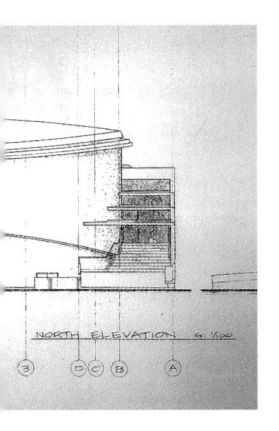

and then left without saying a word. I was astonished by his sketch, as if I saw real magic in front of my face.

I thought this must have been a real "finishing touch". A completely different building appeared there. The ordinary "gas tank" turned into a "concert hall" in an instant.

I could not convince myself it was "because he is a maestro", and I felt depressed the whole day. In the late afternoon of that day, Mr. Raymond called his secretary, Mr. Aoi, and me to his studio-cum-living room and chatted for a little while. Then he left and did not come back. When I looked around, sketches on tracing paper were scattered all over his desk and floor. The massive amount of sketches (nearly one week's worth) were for the elevation plan of the concert hall, and I can still vividly remember the scene. After quite a long time, I understood that he might have noticed my poor English skills and "taught" me by physical experience, rather than by words:

"It took me, at age 82, one week to finally achieve a good plan/design. It is no wonder you couldn't since you are only 22 and have just started. Be patient and stay determined to accomplish the work!"

For 40 years after this incident, it has been my source of energy to overcome obstacles and to solve problems. That was a moment when Mr. Raymond became "my lifetime mentor" as well as my "lifesaver".

Never Compromise!

Around the time when the elevation plan, which almost made me give up being an architect, was almost completed, Junzo Yoshimura visited Mr. Raymond. Before he left, he peeked at the just finished elevation plan, and immediately said, "Don't you think this is better?" as he fixed it with a red marker. He said the 4m diameter sky light, which was in the middle of the round plan, would be better if it had an angle opposite to that of the roof.

Mr. Yoshimura asked, "What do you think, Mr. Raymond?" After a short while, Mr. Raymond said, "Mr. Tsuchiya, I think Mr. Yoshimura's idea is better. Why don't we change it?" The angle of the sky light was instantly changed 180 degrees.

After I calmed down and looked at the plan, it did look better. It is a slightly bitter memory. However, now I remember with nostalgia that it was "just as you would expect" and fun.

Around the time when the design for execution was almost completed with much effort, the chief, Koichi Kitazawa, was going to

んが独立するために退所することになった。突然のことであり、新人の私とレーモンドさんの二人っきりになることに「ガスタンク」立面図とは違った意味で呆然とした。これから、一番大事で難しい現場監理がはじまるのだ。役員会では「誰がこの建築の監理をするのか？」が問題になり、私一人では無理だとの結論になった。当時の事務所の慣例では、レーモンドさんの現場監理は10年以上の経験者がすることになっていた。

　この件がレーモンドさんの耳に入った頃に、また、秘書の葵さんと私がアトリエに呼ばれた。2、3質問してから「君は何歳なんだね？」と聞かれた。「23歳になりました。」しばらくしてから、「私は同じ歳の頃に劇場の大改修の現場を一人でやったよ。」「君も頑張ればできるはずだから、一人でやってみなさい。」とあっさり決まってしまった。

　ただ、大事なこの事だけは守りなさいと一言だけ助言された。「決して妥協してはダメだ！」と。レーモンドさんは初めての現場で、入り口の補強材の梱に施工者の提案の古材を使用することを許可した。そのことを、60年経った今でも後悔しているので、君には同じ思いをさせたくないから……と。

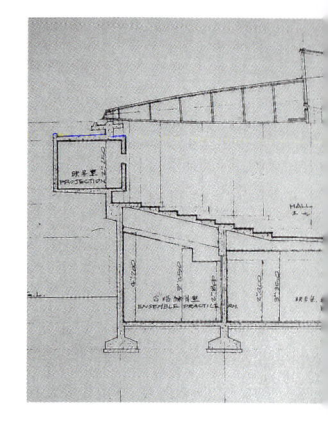

断面図　Section

浮かび上がった十字架

何の予備知識も準備もせずに学芸会の舞台に立った気持ちで現場に乗り込んだ。たいへんな責任の重圧を体中に感じた。

　案の上、現場はまるで猛獣の檻の中だった。施工業者の現場監督やたくさんの荒手の職人たちにさんざんに揶揄を受けた。今でいう「イジメ」である。高所恐怖症の私は、まだ手摺りの設置されていない屋根の足場までつれていかされたり、鉄筋工の職人に直にダメ出しをしたところ、いきなり鉄筋棒で足場パイプを叩きながら現場を2周追いかけられた。ほんとうに殺されるかと思った。冬には足場板が凍っているのに気付かず滑って10メートルの屋根足場から落ちたこともあった。幸い途中の足場に引っかかって軽い打撲ですんではいるが…。

　コンクリート打設時にはすべてが初めての経験であり、コンクリート打設面が綺麗に仕上がるか心配であった。型枠のすべての面を職人と一緒に、軍手に血がにじむまで夢中で叩いて回った。手造りの大きな彫刻をたくさんの人々とつくっているような充実した実感があった。すべてのコンクリート型枠を外

半円はホールのミキサールーム

The semi-circle is an audio mixing room for the concert hall.

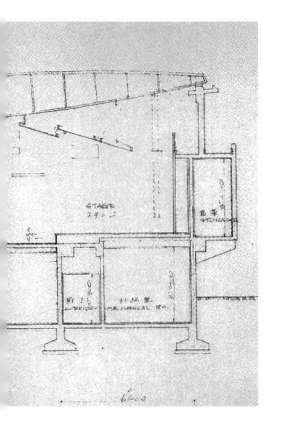

quit in order to start out on his own. It was quite sudden and I was staggered (in a different way from when I was confronted with the "gas tank" elevation plan) by the fact that the team would be only Mr. Raymond and myself. The most important and difficult site supervision was about to start. At the board meeting, "Who is going to supervise this architectural work?" was discussed, and they concluded it was impossible for me to do it alone. According to the office custom at that time, site supervisors for Mr. Raymond's projects should have more than ten years of experience.

When Mr. Raymond heard about this, his secretary Mr. Aoi and I were again called to his studio. After a few questions, he asked, "How old are you?" I said, "I am 23." After a while, he said, "When I was about the same age as you, I supervised a major theater renovation site by myself. It should be possible for you if you try hard, so try." It was quickly decided.

Then he gave me only one piece of advice that was important to follow: "Never compromise!" In Mr. Raymond's first supervisory role, he accepted the builder's suggestion to use secondhand materials for the lintel in the reinforcement material for the entrance. He said he still regretted his decision after 60 years, so he did not want me to have the same experience.

The Projected Cross

I went to the construction site feeling as if I was on a stage at a school art festival without any background knowledge or preparation. I was pressured all over my body by the massive responsibility.

As I had expected, the construction site resembled a cage of beasts. The site supervisor of the contractor and many rough carpenters made much fun of me. It was what is now called "bullying". Someone took me to a roof scaffolding before handrails were installed, though I had acrophobia. When I directly gave a reinforcing-bar worker a few words, he suddenly started chasing me while smacking the scaffolding pipes with a reinforcing bar, and I had to circle the site twice. I thought I was really going to be killed. During winter, I slipped and fell from a ten-meter high roof scaffolding because I did not notice a board on the scaffolding was frozen. Fortunately, I was caught on another scaffold and got away with only a light bruising.

The concrete placement was a completely new experience to me, and I was anxious if the concrete surface would be well formed. With

し、職人も現場員も全員帰った夜にサーチライトを片手に独りで円形ホールの真ん中に立った時、全身が熱くなり、涙が止まらなかった。生まれて初めてえもいえない充実した満足感を味わった。その時以来、建築の楽しさ、素晴らしさを知り、建築は天職であり、ライフワークだという思いが自然と湧いてきた。

　この一年目にした辛い体験は後の現場に立った時にたいへん役にたち、10年以上得をした感じであった。

　殺伐とした毎日の現場で唯一の楽しみは、月に1，2回ほどレーモンド夫妻が2匹の愛犬を連れて現場視察をかねた慰問に来てくれたことである。第1回の視察は、現場内があまりにも汚かったため、1週間の謹慎の指示が現場にでてしまった。作業は何もせずに、全員で掃除の毎日である。工期のないなか、これはほんとうに堪えた。スタート間もない時期だったため、これ以降現場全体に張りつめた緊張感は最後までつづき、素晴らしい出来映えの打放しコンクリートとして表われた。

　レーモンドさんは、この計画過程のすべての場面に私を立ち合わせてくれた。基本設計→実施設計→オーナーへのプレゼン→施工者決定の方法→コストのネゴシエーション→起工式→現場常駐・設計料の集金など→竣工式と。

　竣工式は紅白の垂れ幕もない簡素だが、心のこもった式であった。完成したばかりのホールに先生と生徒全員が集まり、薄暗くしたホールに全員が席に着いた。私は舞台裏へ行き、手動で直径4mのトップライトの4枚の扉を徐々に開いていった時、ホール内から大歓声が湧き上がった。大円形窓の中に十字架が浮かび上がったからだ。続いて校長先生がレーモンド夫妻を紹介し、次に一年間現場で苦労しながら一番頑張ってくれた人と私を紹介してくれた。生徒全員が総立ちで感謝とねぎらいの拍手をしてくれた。この事は生涯忘れることができないほどの感動で、この感動をまた味わいたいと今日まで来てしまった気もする。

　式が終わってほっと一息ついた時、レーモンドさんの爆弾発言があった。「セレモニーで使用した半円形の演台が、この小ホールにはヘビー過ぎてマッチしないから作り直しなさい。」と…。私は困り果てて、仕方なくレーモンドさんのOKサインが入った図面を見せた。すると、一生忘れられないレーモンドさんの言葉があった。

コンクリート打放しの面は美しい

As-cast concrete surface is beautiful.

ホールの十字架が浮かぶトップライト

The sky light of the hall projects a cross.

the builders, I avidly patted all of the surfaces of the formworks until my work gloves were blood-stained. I felt fulfilment as if I was creating a large handmade sculpture with many people. On the night after all of the formworks were removed and all of the carpenters and other people left, I stood alone in the middle of the round hall with a search light in my hand. My entire body became hot and my tears did not stop. For the first time in my life, I tasted indescribable and fulfilling satisfaction. Since then, I came to know the joy and splendor of being an architect. The feeling that architecture is my mission and a desire to make it my lifework naturally occurred in my mind.

The tough experience in my first year was very useful when I supervised other sites afterwards, since it was as if I had gained more than ten years' worth of experience.

The only pleasure from the brutal construction site was Mr. and Mrs. Raymond's consolation and site visits with their two beloved dogs once or twice a month. On the first site visit, a one week suspension was ordered for the site because the site was significantly messy. Each day, everyone just cleaned without doing any other work. It was very hard for us since the construction period was short. This happened only a little while after the construction began. After this incident, the tense atmosphere remained in the entire site until the end, which resulted in a well-made as-cast concrete.

Mr. Raymond allowed me to participate in all steps in this plan process: basic design → design for execution → presentation for the owner → selection of builder → cost negotiation → groundbreaking ceremony → site supervision, collection of design fees, etc. → completion ceremony

The completion ceremony was simple, without even a red and white hanging banner, but it was sincere. In the just-completed and dim-lit hall, all of the teachers and students gathered and were seated. I went backstage and manually opened the four doors of the 4m diameter sky light gradually. Then, a great cheer burst from the hall, because an image of a cross was projected through the large round window. This was followed by an introduction of Mr. and Mrs. Raymond by the principal, and then an introduction of me as the person who had the hardest time and who was the hardest worker during the year of construction. All of the students gave me a standing ovation for thanks and appreciation. This was an unforgettable sensation and I think I have been working until today to achieve the same sensation.

I was relieved after the ceremony ended, but then Mr. Raymond dropped a bombshell on me: "The semi-circle stage that we used for

「僕が悪かった、謝る。僕が買い取るから、作り直してくれないか……。」この一言は、レーモンドさんの仕事に対する厳格、真摯、責任感のある姿勢を表していると思う。「誠実に心から創る」ことであり、これがオーナーから絶大な信頼をえることなのだと。この時以来、OKサインする時は、必ずこの言葉を思い出している。

大きく育った樹木たち

昨年、20年ぶりぐらいに来日中のチェコの建築の学生とクリスチャン・アカデミーを訪れた。当時、高校生だった方にそこで出会った。卒業後、20数年してこの学校が懐かしくなり、当時の職を辞して日本の学校を希望して、今、事務長をされている。当時、私は23歳の現場監理で常駐、事務長のリック・シーリーさんは高校生で同じキャンパスの中で面識はなかったが出会っていたはずである。昔の親友に出会ったような不思議な偶然。これも、レーモンドさんの建築の深さ、豊かさの影響力と思わざるをえない。

敷地内の樹木はできるかぎり残して、建物の配置を決める考えは徹底していた。それはあたかも、その地を永年見つめてきた木の精霊に敬意を表しているかのようである。根底には自然との調和を大事にする哲学がある。

施工業者が配置図通りに地縄張りを完了した。配置図の樹木の位置が正確でなく、建物のラインに樹木がはいっていて困惑していた。レーモンドさんは視察に来て、間髪入れずに建物の位置をずらす指示をだした。

昨年、音楽堂の前に立ちじっくりと見つめた。40年の歳月を経てその樹木がない風景はまったく想像できないくらいに建築と樹が調和している。まるで、樹木が建物を守ってきたようにも見えてきた。

音楽堂の雨落とし

Rainwater drain pipe of the Concert Hall.

the ceremony is too heavy and does not fit in this small hall. Make it again." I was at a loss and reluctantly showed him the plan with the "OK" signature by Mr. Raymond. Then, Mr. Raymond said something I will never forget.

"I was wrong. I'm sorry. I will pay for that one, so please make it again." I believe this phrase represented Mr. Raymond's strict, sincere, and responsible attitude towards work. It was "sincere designing with one's heart", and this attitude gained considerable credibility with the owner. Since then, I always remember this phrase when I sign for approval.

Well-grown Trees

Last year, I visited the Christian Academy for the first time in about 20 years, with architecture students from the Czech Republic who were visiting Japan. There, I met a person who was a high school student when the hall was built. About 20 years after he graduated, he yearned for this school, quit his job, and now works as a general manager in Japan as he wished. Back then, I, at age 23, was a site supervisor and was stationed there, and the general manager Rick Seeley was a high school student. We did not know each other but must have crossed paths somewhere on the campus. It was a mysterious coincidence as if I had met my best friend from the past. I cannot help thinking that it was also due to the effect of the depth and richness of Mr. Raymond's architecture.

He was committed to deciding the arrangement of the buildings by leaving existing trees on the site as much as possible. It was as if he showed his respect for the spirit of the trees, who had watched the site since long ago. A philosophy to cherish harmony with nature existed as a base.

The builder finished stretching a rope on the ground according to the site plan. The location of a tree on the site plan was inaccurate and they were confused because a tree stood inside of the building line. Mr. Raymond came to see it and immediately ordered that the building be shifted.

Last year, I stood in front of the concert hall and looked at it carefully. After 40 years, the building and trees were in harmony and it was impossible to imagine the scenery without these trees. It came to appear as if the trees have been protecting the building.

Antonin Raymond Church & Chapel

		建築名/英語名	竣工年/構造形式	所在地	現存	レーモンド年齢
1		四ツ谷教会 Yotsuya Church/Tokyo/1920	1920 レンガ造	東京都 四ツ谷	失	32才
2		塩釜バプティスト教会 Shiogama Baptist Church/Shiogama/1920	1920 木造	宮城県 塩釜	失	32才
3		青山学院チャペル (内部) Aoyama Gakuin University Chapel/Tokyo/1923	1923 RC造	東京都 青山	失	35才
4		聖ロカ病院チャペル St. Luke's Hospital Chapel/Tokyo/1928	1928 RC造	東京都 築地	現	40才
5		軽井沢 聖パウロカトリック教会 St.Pauls Catholic Church/Karuizawa/1935	1935 木造(一部RC造)	長野県 軽井沢	現	46才
6		東京女子大学礼拝堂 Tokyo Women's Christian College Chapel/Tokyo/1938	1938 RC造	東京都 吉祥寺	現	46才
7		聖ジョセフ教会 Chapel of St.Joseph/Philippines/1949	1949 RC造	フィリピン ネグロス島	現	61才
8		聖アンセルモカトリック目黒教会 St.Anselm's Meguro Church/Tokyo/1954	1954 RC造	東京都 目黒	現	66才
9		聖アルバン教会 St.Alban's Church/Tokyo/1955	1955 木造	東京都 芝	現	67才
10		聖パトリック教会 St.Patrik's Catholic Church/Tokyo/1955	1955 RC造	東京都 豊島	現	67才

	建築名/英語名	竣工年/構造形式	所在地	現存	レーモンド年齢
11	ルーテル教会 Nobeoka Lutheran Church/Nobeoka/1957	1957 木造	宮崎県 延岡	失	69才
12	国際キリスト教大学チャペル (内部) Internation Christian University Chapel/Tokyo/1959	1959 RC造	東京都 三鷹	現	71才
13	聖十字教会 Holycross Anglicanepiscopal Church/Tokyo/1961	1961 木造	東京都 若林	現	73才
14	聖ミカエル教会 St.Michale's Anglicanepiscopal Church/Saporo/1961	1961 木造	北海道 札幌	現	73才
15	立教高校聖パウロ礼拝堂 Rikkyo High School, St.Paul's Chapel/Shiki/1961	1961 RC造	埼玉県 志木	現	73才
16	神言会修道院チャペル Divine Word Seminary Chapel/Tokyo/1963	1963 RC造	東京都 渋谷	現	75才
17	神言神学院チャペル Divine Word Seminary Chapel/Nagoya/1964	1964 RC造	愛知県 名古屋	現	76才
18	カトリック新発田教会 Shibata Catholic Church/Shibata/1965	1965 木造	新潟県 新発田	現	77才
19	立教小学校チャペル Chapel for The Rikkyo Primary School/Tokyo/1967	1967 RC造	東京都 池袋	現	79才

World Architecture

Antonin Raymond
Church & Chapel
Japan

Text | 内藤恒方 ないとうつねかた
建築家・ランドスケープアーキテクト。1934年生まれ　東京芸術大学建築学科卒業後、レーモンド設計事務所勤務。カリフォルニア大学大学院修了後、ササキ・ドーソン・ディメイ・アソシエイツ勤務、ニューヨーク州立大学助教授を経て帰国。ALP設計室を主宰。

Text | 土屋重文 つちやしげふみ
建築家。1947年生まれ　日本大学理工学部建築学科卒業後、レーモンド設計事務所入所、A・レーモンドに3年間師事。現在、同事務所の取締役。作品に川俣町立川俣南小学校、キープ協会「清泉寮新館」など多数。

Photos | 宮本和義
写真家。1941年上海生まれ。1964年から建築、旅のフィールドで撮影活動を開始。建築、まちなみ、仏像の名手。著書に「ワールドアーキテクチャー・シリーズ」(バナナブックス)、『近代建築再見』(エクスナレッジ)、『古寺彩彩』(JTB)、『近代建築散歩』(小学館)など多数。

Text | Tsunekata Naito
Architect/ Landscape architect. Born in 1934. After graduating from Tokyo University of the Arts, Naito worked for Raymond Architectural Design Office. He came back to Japan to establish ALP design office after the master course at the graduate school of University of California, working for Sasaki Dawson Demay Associates, and associate professor at State University of New York.

Text | Shigefumi Tsuchiya
Architect. Born in 1947. Tsuchiya joined Raymond Architectural Design Office and worked under A. Raymond for 3 years and he is now a board member of the office. His major works include Kawamata-minami Elementary School founded by Kawamata town and New Seisen-Ryo in KEEP Foundation.

Photos | Kazuyoshi Miyamoto
Photographer. Born in Shanghai in 1941.
Since 1964, he has been taking architectural and travel photographs. He is thoroughly accomplished at his photographs of architecture, streetscape and Buddhist statues. His major books include "World architecture"(banana books), "Reviet modern architecture" (X-knowledge Co., Ltd.) "Colorful old temples" (JTB Corp.) and "Walk in modern architecture" (Shogakukan Inc.).

写真 | 宮本和義 ©
執筆 | 内藤恒方　土屋重文 ©
翻訳 | 牧尾晴喜 [スタジオ OJMM] ©
　　　ガンター倫子、ケネス・ガンター
編集 | 石原秀一
デザイン | マルプデザイン
印刷・製本 | モリモト印刷株式会社
制作協力 | レーモンド設計事務所
　　　　　軽井沢聖パウロカトリック教会
　　　　　聖アンセルモカトリック目黒教会
　　　　　神言神学院
　　　　　クリスチャン・アカデミー日本校
　　　　　聖十字教会

Photos | © Kazuyoshi Miyamoto
Text | © Thunekata Naitou, Shigebumi Thuthiya
Translation | © Haruki Makio [Studio OJMM]
　　　　　　　Michiko Gunter, Kenneth Gunter
Chief Editor | Shuichi Ishihara
Design | Malpu Design Co.,Ltd.
Printer | MORIMOTO PRINT Co.,Ltd.
Special Thanks | Raymond Architectural Design Office
　　　　　　　　St. Paul's Catholic Church
　　　　　　　　Meguro Catholic Church
　　　　　　　　Divine Word Seminary
　　　　　　　　Christian Academy in Japan
　　　　　　　　Holycross Anglicanepiscopal Church

アントニン・レーモンド
チャーチ&チャペル
日本

2013年10月10日　第1刷発行　　　　First printing October 10, 2013

編集者 | 石原秀一　　　　　　　　Chief Editor | Shuichi Ishihara
発行者 | 工藤秀之　　　　　　　　Publisher | Hideyuki Kudo
発行所 | バナナブックス ©　　　　© Banana Books
　　　　株式会社トランスビュー　　TRANSVIEW Co.,Ltd.

〒103-0007　東京都中央区日本橋浜町2-10-1-2F　　2-10-1-2F, Nihonbashi-Hamacho Chuo-ku, Tokyo, 103-0007 Japan
Tel. 03-3664-7334　Fax. 03-3664-7335　　Tel.+81-3-3664-7334　Fax.+81-3-3664-7335
http://www.transview.co.jp/　　　　　　　http://www.transview.co.jp/

2013 BananaBooks, Printed in Japan
All rights reserved
ISBN978-4-902930-28-3